2/23

D0622038

PSYCHOLOGY AND THE CROSS

Fr. G. Emmett Carter

PSYCHOLOGY AND THE CROSS

SOPHIA INSTITUTE PRESS
Manchester, New Hampshire

Copyright © 2022 by Sophia Institute Press

Originally published by Bruce Publishing Company, Milwaukee, in 1959. For this 2022 edition by Sophia Institute Press, a few words have been replaced to update the language for a modern context.

Printed in the United States of America. All rights reserved.

Cover design: Updatefordesign Studio

Nihil Obstat:
Rev. John McConnell
Vice–Chancellor
Censor ad hoc

Imprimatur:
Lawrence P. Whalen, V.G.
Auxiliary Bishop of Montreal
November 10, 1958

Scripture quotations are taken from the Douay-Rheims edition of the Old and New Testaments.

No part of this book may be reproduced, stored in a retrieval system, or transmitted in any form, or by any means, electronic, mechanical, photocopying, or otherwise, without the prior written permission of the publisher, except by a reviewer, who may quote brief passages in a review.

Sophia Institute Press
Box 5284, Manchester, NH 03108
1-800-888-9344
www.SophiaInstitute.com

Sophia Institute Press is a registered trademark of Sophia Institute.

paperback ISBN 978-1-64413-786-4

ebook ISBN 978-1-64413-787-1

Library of Congress Control Number: 2022943477

First printing

Dedication

To my sisters,
Sr. Mary Lenore, S.P.,
Past President of the Ontario Teacher's Federation
and
Rev. Mother M. Carter, R.S.C.J.,
Convent of the Sacred Heart, Winnipeg, Man.,
who so well exemplify in their dealing with youth
the "meeting of the ways,"
this book is affectionately and gratefully dedicated.

CONTENTS

• • •

Section One
To Man's Estate

Section Two
The Outgoing Self

Section Three
The Psychological Import of Christian Idealism

Section Four
Fear

*"True psychology without metaphysical bias or
theological prejudice walks hand in hand with ascetical
wisdom and the religious guidance of souls."*

PUBLISHER'S NOTE TO THE 1959 EDITION

● ● ●

This fundamental and penetrating volume gives a new insight into
the relation of the teaching of the Catholic Church to the theories
of psychology, presenting a well–rounded picture of how contem-
porary psychology can aid the Christian. Fr. Carter explains that
it is essential to integrate the teachings of Christianity with the
findings of modern psychology if the latter is to attain its goal. This
goal, the proper development of the ego, is in complete accord with
Christian teaching and can be clearly visualized only in the light
of the Faith, since only Christianity fully respects the dignity of
the human person.

This lucid and vigorous book bears witness to the fact that many
of the things that are apparently being discovered today in psychology have already been taught by the Church; e.g., the psychological
concept of "community" is in accord with and must be fulfilled in
the Christian notion of solidarity. The author also points out that
it is essential to integrate Christian ideals, such as humility, along
with the valuable concepts of modern psychology in the training
and development of the human person. A thorough understanding of the connection between religion and psychology, the author
insists, will lead to the maturity that is the meeting place of the true

man and the true Christian. Writing with ease, clarity, and candor, Fr. Carter explores all phases of personal life and scrutinizes man's need for self–comprehension and self–expression. He examines the Freudian triad, the id, ego, and super–ego, in the light of both Christian and psychological truths, and provides a brief and accurate analysis of the metaphysical biases during the age of Freud that caused him to hold erroneous positions on the nature of man, the idea of God, and religion. Not only does the author clearly label the errors committed by Freud, but he shows how to utilize what is valid in his teachings and points out what can be incorporated into the Christian view of man and human life. For example, many of Freud's observations on the nature of fear are in perfect accord with the Christian concept of man's fall from a preternatural state.

All interested in the relation of religion to psychology and the education of youth, especially parents and teachers, will find this book of particular value. Fr. Emmett Carter, a renowned Canadian educator, was founding director of St. Joseph Teacher's College in Montreal.

Preface to the 1959 Edition

• • •

Our inveterate habits of intellectual isolation and of mistrust for anything new, our tendencies to enclose in airtight compartments the natural and the supernatural and the disciplines that deepen our understanding of them, have so fashioned our minds that we are not surprised by the spectacle of things occupying parallel lines without any apparent possibility of meeting or of collaborating. Thus, we cannot help being agreeably surprised and happy to discover an author who has not been afraid to combat these unfortunate tendencies and who has had the courage to write a volume in which disciplines apparently as divergent, not to say antagonistic, as depth psychology and Christian theology walk hand in hand, not on parallel roads, but along the same pathways. We are indebted to Fr. Emmett Carter for this initiative, and we should be grateful to him for having undertaken it and for having brought it to a happy conclusion.

This short volume with the somewhat enigmatic title, *Psychology and the Cross*, develops the following theme: Modern psychology in spite of its amoral and non–Christian origins is a wonderful instrument for bringing the Christian to an awareness of all that is profoundly human in our revealed religion. Modern psychology is a powerful light that comes to confirm, in and by a profound analysis

of human conduct, the most elementary and also the most fundamental truths of the Gospel. Nor is it surprising that this should be
the case, because God is the Creator of all truth, precisely because
He is the Creator of being and of the intelligence that knows being. What is surprising is that we should have had to wait so long
to begin a true collaboration between the truths that come directly
to us from our Father and those that His children unearth with so
much difficulty.

Everything is not true in the discoveries of modern psychology,
and the hypotheses that are at the basis of certain of its theories
should be criticized and sometimes rejected. But it remains true
that depth psychology has brought to light hitherto unknown
secrets of the enslavement that lies at the level of the human unconscious and that it has invented methods that permit man to
examine this newly discovered dimension of his emotional life and
to see the continuous relationship between the unconscious and
his daily living. In the Bible God has told us that man, although
created for immortality, for joy and happiness, for freedom in
the good pursued with love — that this man has become a sinner.
When the Bible tells us this, it does not describe the mechanism
of this slavery that is sin; the Bible does not give us the *how* of this
progressively all–encompassing subjection from which humanity
suffers; the Bible does, however, reveal to us the *why* of this slavery,
of these lies that are our lives, of this agony that penetrates the
life of man and takes away his joy: sin — that of our first parents,
those of our forebears and often our own personal sins — is the
why of the slavery of tortured human nature. On the other hand,
psychology gives us the answer to the *how;* it describes the birth of
what it calls inhibitions, repressions, complexes, a set of terms that
designates the same profound sickness of our being, the disorder
that entered in when we turned our backs on God.

What is more normal than that a doctrine that knows why man suffers, why he is sick, why he dies, why he is disoriented, should take, not as its guide, but as its traveling companion a discipline that is capable of analyzing the symptoms of our disorders and of our slavery and that offers a means to uncover the symptoms even when they escape consciousness with a view of bringing them to the level of consciousness? In accordance with our sound Christian doctrine, we know that all the realm of morality is a realm of the conscious. Our responsibility has its roots in choice, in a dynamic freedom, and in our dominion over our acts and the objects toward which they are directed. At the same time, psychology offers to Christians this magnificent instrument by which we can be made aware of the totally unknown part of man, and that permits us, consequently, to project upon this unknown territory the light of faith and of supernatural prudence.

It is precisely this supernatural light of faith and of prudence that Canon Carter casts on the principal themes that are at the base of psychology and psychoanalysis. In the light of this vision, he shows how much better equipped is the religion of Christ to cure these ills from which we suffer once we have come to know them, or to prevent these tragedies in the human beings who are confided to our care. Thus, the concept of "community" as developed by the psychologist enlightens Christian solidarity, that we know under the name of the Mystical Body. But on the other hand, this latter concept gives a meaning and a strength to the former that leaves far behind the fumbling notions of ends and motivations that are the unaided findings of the "psychological community." In the same fashion, the emulation, the imitation, the sublimation that psychology proposes to man and that he uses to re–establish lost equilibrium or unstable emotional balance help to manifest the meaning of basic Christian charity. But this charity, by carrying the ideal up to the very limits of divine perfection, by proposing to man the vision of being the image of the Father by living in the imitation of Christ, and by giving to Christians the inner vitality to realize this ideal, creates an atmosphere of selfless giving that both realizes and surpasses all the hopes of the natural psychologist. And how limited is the immunity against fear and anxiety conferred by psychological doctrine compared to the security that one receives in the Christian view of the universe created by the Father, redeemed by the Incarnate Son of the same Father, and governed by the loving and merciful wisdom of this Christ who came on earth solely to teach us to be happy as children of God in circumstances that at times seem very far removed from happiness and joy.

The aim of depth psychology is to know man better in order to develop his maturity. But Christianity, placing constantly before our eyes the human ideal made to the image of God and destined to be free to love as God loves, cannot fail to produce this maturity of man, a maturity that is in balance, adapted socially to the circumstances of life in peace and in joy. In a word, the Christian life produces the completely virtuous man, because supernature does not destroy nature but is its best hope in the work of human education that is the development of the true adult.

All these themes are developed in a simple, vigorous, and even at times humorous style; and they lead to this conclusion: "True Psychology without metaphysical bias or theological prejudice walks hand in hand with ascetical Wisdom and the religious guidance of souls."

May the reading of Canon Carter's book give to all of those who are interested in the education of children or of youth the desire to know all the truth that psychology teaches concerning human reality, so that, in using these truths, they may find greater ease and skill in leading to maturity those who are confided to their care. Only in this maturity will we find the meeting place of the true man and the true Christian.

L. M. Régis, O.P.
Dean of the Faculty of Philosophy
University of Montreal

November 30, 1958
The feast of St. Andrew who died on the cross for the love of Christ

INTRODUCTION

· · ·

In the days of my youth, when under the impulse of God's grace, my path turned toward a life of dedication to the service of the Church, I decided that God was calling me to the diocesan priesthood. To me the greatest possible calling was that of the immediate service of souls. Who could ask for anything greater, anything more noble, anything more important than the administration of the sacraments, and the immediate person–to–person contact that exists between the parish priest and the souls committed to his care?

Yes, it was this form of ministry for me, and all through the seminary my thoughts turned in this direction. In the particular diocese where I was born and grew up there was not much opportunity for the English–speaking clergy to become "specialists" in any given field, and so I was convinced that of all the sure things in the world this was the surest, that I should spend my years working in the parish ministry. A succession of "specialists" addressed us during our seminary days. I listened, carefully I hope, but with a somewhat distracted ear, because education, social service, administration—none of these things were for me.

Alas for my illusions. The good Lord must have watched my assumptions with a mildly amused air. In any case my first appointment was to education. I have been in this field in almost all its ramifications ever since. But it was not long before I learned another lesson. There is "a difference of ministries but one Lord." Moreover, there is only one human race and souls are everywhere. The same kindly understanding that I had admired so much in the priests I had known needed to be found in *those who* taught and in those who shaped the lives of little children. The same work was to be done, although in a different manner.

It was then that I began to fall in love with the idea of using every possible resource, natural and supernatural, to bring children to God. My educational research followed these lines as did my work for the necessary academic qualification. And, as so often happens, in the background was the urge to share, if possible, a little of the light that had been given to me in abundance and of which I hoped I had conserved a few rays.

This is the story of why I have tried to write about *Psychology and the Cross*. As I shall try to explain in my first chapter, it is an attempt to bring together the tremendous, the vital findings of modern psychology with the age–old wisdom of the Church's teaching concerning the relationships between God and man.

The core of this book was written over ten years ago and it is thanks to the patience and perception of The Bruce Publishing Company that it is now seeing the light of day. My debt of course is to everything I have read, but above all to the people whom I have known. This is not really an a priori position. I have not started with principles in order that they may find their application in people. I truly began with people and saw in their actions the results of deeply rooted principles.

It was my great fortune early in life to make contact with a dedicated class of people: the religious and lay Catholic teacher. Here I saw the attempt to bring together the true understanding of the child, that means an attempt to penetrate into his complex nature and at the same time to realize that that nature is also a super–nature. Therefore, my first debt is to the teachers who put up with my early efforts and from whom I learned so much.

There is also in my native city an organization that I feel to be unique. I refer to the Thomas More Institute for Adult Education. Here, too, I have learned to seek for the solution of the problem of reaching the totality of man. This is one group in which there are no professors or administrators but only "learners."

My fifteen years in Newman Club work has also been a fertile source of inspiration and I hope of some wisdom. To see the youth of our country in direct contact with the problems of the intellect as well as those of living does give an insight into psychology as well as a better understanding of the need of the application of the supernatural.

In detail and with considerable fear of omission I wish to express my acknowledgments to His Excellency, Bishop Whelan, Auxiliary Bishop of Montreal, and to Rev. John McConnell, Vice–Chancellor of the Archdiocese, for their intelligent reading of the manuscript and for valuable suggestions along the lines of theological clarity; to Dr. Karl Stern, who from his busy schedule took the necessary time to go over the text and to make valuable suggestions and amendments; to Rev. Eric O'Connor, S.J., and Miss Charlotte Tansey, the "mainsprings" of the Thomas More Institute, for their help on a number of questions; to Mr. Erwin Geissman, one of the editors of *Cross Currents,* for valuable help; to Dr. Thomas Francoeur and to Mrs. C. Murin for reading the manuscript and giving their valuable opinions; and to my secretaries, Mrs. T. Hughes, Mrs. Jean Mackinnon, Miss Carole Lomasney, and Miss Catherine Farrell not only for their help but for their patience in working on the script at those odd moments that of necessity I had to employ in order to do this work.

Montreal, P.Q., November 9, 1958.

SECTION ONE
TO MAN'S ESTATE

CHAPTER 1
THE MEETING OF THE WAYS

● ● ●

There is an interesting, though perhaps apocryphal, story about Christopher Columbus. It appears that after Columbus had returned home there was the usual belittling of his exploits. One day during a meal an acquaintance was holding forth about the fact that the concept that the world was round was not a new one, and that anyone could have made the discoveries that Columbus had made. Columbus listened courteously and after a while took a hard–boiled egg from a plate and passed it to the long–winded orator. Columbus said, "My friend, are you able to make this egg stand up on its end by itself?" The man tried several times without success and finally gave up with a laugh, saying, "It is obviously impossible." Columbus took the egg, broke the shell at the point slightly, and sat it on the table. He smiled at his critical acquaintance and said, "You see, it is quite simple; it is only necessary to have thought of it."

Columbus might have added that "discoveries" usually do not mean thinking of a thing for the first time. They often mean solely that someone has thought through to a conclusion what many have been thinking about vaguely at previous moments. Hans Selye, in his now famous work on stress, points out the same fact. He shows conclusively that the concept of stress was not one that he had invented; indeed, it had been in the minds of many men for many years. His merit was in taking it out and holding it up for all to see. He thought through what many had vaguely perceived.

In the realm of modern psychology there is much that is analogous to this idea of discovery. Karl Stern, in his excellent work on the relationship between psychiatry and religion, describes the development of modern psychology as "The Third Revolution." Now revolution is by definition "a turning over." It is not the invention of something new. It is not even a discovery. It is taking something that already exists and turning it, as it were, upside down. If this change was needed, then we presume the right side comes uppermost. However, in human affairs things are seldom that simple. Generally, it is not a question of black and white but an intermediary color — or perhaps a whole series of colors. Psychology touches on so many human values and human considerations that it is impossible for it to reach a conclusion without much evolution, not to say revolution, and without many false starts and half–truths.

The name of Sigmund Freud is, of course, synonymous with modern psychology. He is one of the most controversial figures in history for reasons that we will examine later. For the moment let us be content to look briefly at the work that this man has achieved. Before him there was, obviously, psychology. The operation of the human mind and, indeed, its connection with the human body, had always been an object of speculation. For our purpose it is sufficient to point out that the earliest history of man indicates his concern with those interworkings of his psychic self. One of the most ancient of all authenticated writings, the Bible, contains in its very first book a statement that invites us to psychological speculation: "Let us make man in our own image and likeness" (Gen. 1:26). Here is a blueprint for the study of man's psychic forces as at least an analogy with those that we must find in the great Spirit. And the quest that is begun here continues through the ages.

Before Freud perhaps the most generally known type of psychology is what is called today rational or philosophical psychology, that was centered about man's conscious activities and sought to discover the ultimate principles of his life as a rational animal. But as time went on, and as more and more was known of the actual workings of man's inner being on an observable level, scientific psychology, as it is called, came more and more to the fore. Scientists began to examine and to weigh and to test man's reactions to various situations. Animal psychology helped to establish an analogy. Ways and means were invented to produce and measure the reaction of man to many circumstances. Hypnosis and suggestion, for example, were findings that predated Freud.

On the medical side, the nineteenth century witnessed outstanding research on the relationships between mind and body, leading to a better understanding of such relationships. The problem was being set up and considered. But none of this detracts from the genius of the man who first perceived the key to much of what was in the depth of man's inner personality. This man was Sigmund Freud. His work was to have the most far–reaching consequences upon human history, and the direction that he gave to human thinking may well have been one of the most important natural happenings the world has ever known.

It is far from our purpose to write a treatise on "the life and work of Sigmund Freud." This has been done, and very effectively, by far more competent persons. But a brief study of some of the outstanding problems raised by Freud is necessary for our further considerations. Everyone, psychologist and layman alike, is familiar with the terminology that has come from Freud and that has been developed by his followers and disciples. It is practically impossible to go to a play, to listen to a discourse on almost any subject, or even at times to attend a sporting event, without running into words like inhibition, fixation, or complex. That these terms or, at any rate, many of the more difficult ones are often misused, is true. But enough of their meaning has rubbed off into our daily language to make psychology a science of every man. Practically every field of human endeavor has been affected by this new knowledge. Medical science in all its facets, education, and even such diverse fields as advertising, warfare, sports, and amusements, have all received an imprint from this tremendous development of the past century.

All of this is fortunate and good inasmuch as man is called to perfect himself in every way possible. What is less fortunate is that the basis of many of these concepts has very often been misunderstood, and where there is general knowledge there is also, very often, general ignorance or confusion.

There is a controversy among psychologists as to the most important of the Freudian contributions. For a long time it was believed that his sex theory was the great discovery and the great key to the psychic kingdom. This sex concept might be described by saying that Freud maintained that virtually all of the hidden drives of man were of sexual genesis or derivation. In a world where sex is commercialized and misdirected as blatantly as in ours, this was a concept to feed the minds of the prurient or of those whose sole consideration was gain. As a result, there was, in our opinion, an overemphasis on this concept and its importance to the Freudian system. Without wishing to give judgment in this matter, we think it is safe to say that most, if not all, modern psychologists even of the psychoanalytic school do not follow Freud in the total reaches of his original sexual theory. There can be no doubt about the value of his concept but it does not seem to be the central one.

What seems to be emerging as the very center of the whole Freudian system and, as a result, of the whole of modern psychology is the concept of the *unconscious*. Up to the time of Freud, man was very well aware that not all of his psychic forces were on the surface. Sometimes these hidden drives or these flashes of inspiration or of memory or of what was called intuition were treated either as diabolical or angelical inspirations. Some knowledge of the existence of telepathy was known and discussed, but it was not until Freud that a carefully analyzed and comprehensive theory of the unconscious was developed.

Hand in hand with this concept of the unconscious is the famous Freudian triad of the *id,* the *ego,* and the *super–ego.* Since some readers may not be entirely familiar with this terminology, a brief description may be helpful.

The best of many analogies to the id, the ego, and the super–ego is Freud's own description in terms of a child. When we contemplate a very young baby, we see what we might call nature in the raw. The child's drives are right on the surface. When he is hungry he announces the fact to the world in screams that will rapidly become cries of rage if he is too long frustrated. Pain and discomfort of any kind meet with the same treatment. He is not, as we say, inhibited. He manifests whatever he feels without hesitation and without reserve. With this wild drive, if he were physically strong enough, he would attack anything in his way with an aggressiveness that would be murderous. If sex urges were present, they would be of a maniacal variety. The child exercises no control over his drives.

Fortunately for the human race, there are mechanisms that allow for adjustment and adaptation. As the child grows he begins to realize that he cannot manifest these drives. External forces are greater than he, and he learns that it is to his profit to wait, to put up with, to accept. But according to Freud the drives are still there. These raw drives are what he describes as the "id." This has been termed the core of the unconscious. According to modern psychology the id is there at all stages of life. It is not something that we can destroy or eliminate. It is simply the existence of primitive urges that are completely neutral and (for once we may use the term correctly) amoral. Therefore, they are neither good nor bad; they are beyond the reach of morality inasmuch as they are not under the control of either reason or will. They are simply drives in the same way that water rushing down a hill is a drive. How they are harnessed and for what purpose is another question.

But let us return to our child. The newborn babe is not conscious of himself as a separate entity. He is conscious only of those forces that are acting upon him. He has not yet reached the point where he can reflect upon himself and, therefore, discover the need for curbs. As he develops, two things take place. First, he becomes conscious of himself as a separate and governable being; second, he realizes that he cannot achieve everything he wishes. This introduces us to the second Freudian concept, that of the ego.

The term *ego* has a variety of meanings in psychology. But in its most simple sense it means the essentially conscious and sensible part of the mind in which we have, as it were, our rational selves. It has been said that there are three selves in each of us. The one we think we are, the one that others think we are, and the one that we really are. To describe the Freudian position the first of these would probably be the most effective. It is our self–consciousness; it is the same person who governs our lives. It is the ego of which we are conscious. When we realize that our drives are leading us into danger or into an area where we should not go, we control them, divert them, or guide them. Sometimes we repress them completely. All of this, of course, is on the conscious level. Underneath the surface the drives are always there, always pushing; and, as we will see, sometimes they manifest themselves in devious ways, for example, in dreams. In these circumstances, since they are repressed and come up unbidden, they usually arise in a disguise.

And what of the third of these three concepts, the super–ego? The analogy with the child is a little more difficult here. However, many psychologists have expressed it in terms of the relationship of a young person to a maiden aunt. Still others describe it as conscience. But to anyone trained in the *philosophia perennis* this will only arouse difficulties. The main thing to remember is that the super–ego, like the id, is within the unconscious. It sets up standards of performance that are not appreciated or realized by the conscious ego. These, indeed, may have been established within us by our environment without our realization. These too in a sense are drives, but they are drives for a type of perfection. They are standards that affect us unconsciously; we believe we must live up to them although we have no realization, perhaps, of this "perfectionist" aspiration within us.[1]

The stage is now set for some understanding of the unconscious and its effects. Outside the range of consciousness there are two sets of tensions: one the blind force of nature urging us without our knowledge to express ourselves in whatever way the drive of the moment may inspire; the other a set of tensions based upon standards that are imposed upon us, perhaps, by a parental upbringing or other environmental forces. Hence it is not surprising that the result should often be conflict. This conflict will manifest itself in ways that may not be at all familiar to us and that may take much analysis before we realize its origin or its meaning. A few very simple and very standard examples will suffice.

One is the mother who on the conscious level thinks she is sacrificing everything for her son. Working for him day and night and insisting on repairing all his mistakes, paying his bills, and supporting him in all his difficulties, she may, in fact, be responding to

---

[1] This does not necessarily mean true perfection but perhaps an entirely false and artificial level of attainment or conduct. Unconscious prudery or snobbery may be of the "super–ego."

an unconscious urge to dominate her son and to keep him tied to her. Or again, a man may "freeze up" and be unable to go forward in a certain direction in his life because the super–ego is telling him that he is doing the wrong thing in bettering the record set by his father. Freudian "slips," saying the wrong word, forgetting things, are all possible manifestations of the unconscious.

It is true that much of this has been exaggerated, and at times ludicrous errors have been made by universalizing the concept of the unconscious. For example, people have been known to state that whenever you leave an object behind you unintentionally it is a sign that you did not want to leave, or that all students who choose seats near the door are unconsciously antisocial. But, at the same time, it is undeniable that this concept is valid and will stand up to the test of experience.

However, we would ask the reader to keep these limitations in mind because much of the purpose of this work is to try to help with motivation that is, by definition, not on the level of the unconscious. However, it is premature for us, at this moment, to establish the juxtaposition. Another consideration awaits us, namely, the metaphysical conflicts that unfortunately have been introduced into modern psychology.

Metaphysical Background of Modern Psychology

God works in His own ways. Hence it is venturesome, to say the least, for us to say that anything is "unfortunate." However, we must judge things as human history unfolds them before our eyes, and with the proper reservation we can say that it was most unfortunate that Sigmund Freud was born at the time and in the place where he was. The mid–nineteenth century in central Europe was not the best place in the world for the development of religious idealism. It was an extraordinary period. Man was in the throes of his most important scientific discoveries. There was a neo–humanism abroad and a false rationalism. Man was once more convinced that he could do it all by himself. The faith of the Middle Ages had gone through the crucible of both the Renaissance and the Reformation, and had come out purified in many ways, but certainly not universalized. In the Western World the Protestant Revolt was now having its effect. The idea that every man is a conscience to himself, however high–sounding and attractive, was open to the most exaggerated interpretation and this it had received. It meant very quickly that man was not a conscience to himself, but rather a god to himself. Consequently, the concepts of a transcendent God and of religion were receding from the minds of men in this scientific era of discovery.

The famous story of Pasteur is so well known it hardly bears repetition. To many of his contemporaries it was a strange anomaly that he should be a great scientist and, at the same time, have "the faith of a Brittany peasant." His famous reply was that he hoped some day to be a sufficiently great scientist to have also the faith of a Brittany peasant's wife. But Pasteur, as is indicated by the very existence of the story, was an exception. At this period of history it was normal that people should have been astounded to see a great scientist also a great believer.

Thus, Sigmund Freud was born into an era and an area where science and religion were not considered as having any relationship or even any possible acquaintanceship. Freud, for that matter, was a very strange man himself. He was full of gullible superstition. His most laudatory biographers have pointed out the strange conduct that he held on many occasions. Thus his religious ignorance is not too surprising. But it is, nevertheless, a fact. Freud was not a philosopher. He was much less a theologian. So, unfortunately, he did not understand the distinction between the realms of positive science, of philosophy, and theology, and he seemed to think that his qualifications as an outstanding scientist made him also an authority on philosophy and theology. Some texts in which he begins to indulge his fantasies about race theories and his explanation of some of man's drives in terms of his history are a strange commentary on the ignorance of the great. The depth of his philosophical knowledge may be gauged somewhat by the following quotation from his *Moses and Monotheism:* "Primitive people come to the peculiarly dualistic conception on which the animistic system rests by observing the phenomena of sleep, and death that resembles sleep, and through the effort to explain these conditions."[2] He doesn't seem to have any other knowledge of the basis on which the philosophers of yesterday and today accept the theory of a spiritual soul. In the same work he calls "the creation of demons and spirits" the first theoretical accomplishment of man.[3]

His pronouncements as a theologian are equally astounding: "It would be different if demons really existed, but we know that like gods they are really only the product of the psychic powers of man. They have been created out of something."[4] In other words, Freud has man creating God instead of vice versa. When he writes of Christianity, he writes almost invariably of the Christian "myth." One of his most famous theological concepts is the inference that the idea of the Incarnation grew from the primitive murder of the father of the tribe by the sons to gain possession of his wives and of his power.

But since none of this is backed up by other than the most superficial statements, there is hardly any use in dealing with it. We

---

[2]   Sigmund Freud, *Moses and Monotheism* (New York: Alfred A. Knopf, 1939), p. 133.

[3]   *Ibid.,* p. 162.

[4]   *Ibid.,* p. 43.

quote these things only to show that Freud was laboring under a bias. We can afford to be a little more charitable than Freud, and, in effect, credit him with ignorance. Here is what he says about the Incarnation and the Redemption directly, "that a man should become a God and that a God should die ... today seems an outrageous proposition...."[5] In *Totem and Taboo,* he makes the most outstanding of his theological blunders since he mixes up the concepts of the Immaculate Conception and the Virgin Birth. He writes as follows: "Though they raise the myth of Immaculate Conception through a spirit to a general theory of conception, we cannot for that reason credit them with ignorance as to the conditions of procreation, any more than we could the old races who lived during the rise of the Christian myths."[6]

We are not trying to lessen the appreciation of Freud's contribution by exposing his theological ignorance. It was unfortunate that Freud did not himself understand the separation in these various fields and recognize that he could very well have established all his scientific research and achieved all the goals that he set for himself without attacking either philosophy or Christianity. That he did not do so was as much a commentary on the spirit of the times as upon his own basic ignorance of the subject. During the period in which he lived it was thought that science and religion were in a death struggle and that one could not survive if the other did. This view, that is truly a myth, has been laid by the heels long since, and scientists and theologians today live in relative peace and mutual respect even though they do not always think alike when their subjects touch.

What is important for our consideration is that because of this metaphysical bias, that was picked up by Freud's disciples and

[5] *Totem and Taboo,* p. 259.
[6] *Ibid.,* p. 206.

successors, psychology itself, and in particular, psychoanalysis was given a bad name. It is true that in the individual psychology of Adler, in which the sexual theory was largely left aside and the concept of the individual and more conscious reaction[7] was introduced, there was not the same type of attack upon religion. Moreover, Jung has actually introduced religion into his psychological theories and made it a part of their essence. His widely quoted statement that "everyone of my patients in the second–half of life, that is over thirty–five, fell ill because he had lost that which the living religions of every age had given their followers; and none of them has really been healed who did not regain his religious outlook,"[8] indicates the extent to which he has returned to the concept of the necessity of religious therapy along with psychotherapy. At the same time, most psychologists for a long period tended rather to follow the anti-religious views of Freud. Some still do.

As a result, a most unfortunate conflict arose and still is having its effects in our day. It was felt that no one could be simultaneously a good Christian, or even a true believer, and a good psychologist. Some of the early psychoanalysts (generally speaking, there is much greater discretion in our times) prescribed releases that were contrary to Christian morality from tension and from anxieties produced by *basic* drives. Thus, on the dual front of dogma and morals, a very unfortunate impression was given.

On the other hand, a failure to understand and to study the findings of psychology led a number of theologians, both professional and amateur, to treat lightly or even to condemn the teaching of psychology. This has been righted in our time by the official statements

---

[7]   Particularly, the concept of inferiority feeling that is much more on the conscious level than Freud's anxieties.

[8]   *Modern Man in Search of a Soul* (London: Routledge and Kegan Paul, 1953), p. 264.

of Pope Pius XII and by his appeal for true Christians, particularly true Christian scholars, to engage in the field of psychology, and to extract therefrom the highest amount of benefit and truth. And that brings us precisely to the task at hand.

The Unity of Truth

What we all need to realize is that God is the God of Truth. There cannot be truths in one field that contradict truths in another field. Truth is one. Also, there is no legitimate field of human investigation that is closed to the Christian. On the contrary, there is a marriage of truths in which one field can derive the greatest good from the knowledge of the other. Thus, it is true to say that psychology can draw immense strength from the truths of Christianity, particularly the ascetical truths that have been practiced by the saints down the ages. On the other hand, a greater knowledge of supernatural truth can be achieved through a greater knowledge of psychology. Ours is a revealed religion. By this we mean that we have not discovered the truth in this field as in other fields by unaided human investigation. The central truths of our religion have come to us from God. But when He said, "Let us make man in our own image and likeness," He did not decree an amorphous, dull, lifeless being. He meant to give to man a part of His own dynamism and even a participation in His own self–determination. Under God man is meant to be a providence to himself. Even in the intellectual sphere man is meant to evolve the truths of religion and to penetrate their meaning more and more as his mind is clarified through the succeeding ages. As a result, when a natural truth, like the truth of psychology, comes to him, it is not only his right but his duty to make use of it for a greater understanding of the truths of religion.

In the following pages we shall attempt to make something of a liaison between these two areas. However, in order to avoid error, it is necessary to point out immediately that we are not dealing directly with the psychoanalytic problems of the unconscious. By very definition these are things that have to be reached by a different kind of therapy. Since we will occasionally refer to this therapy throughout this book, it may be of some value to describe it briefly even though superficially. The treatment of anxiety or of any tension that comes from the unconscious must be done by the professional psychologist. The psychoanalyst goes about it by trying to present to the patient the scheme of things within him. As we have mentioned, the drives that are repressed reappear in disguised form. The psychoanalyst examines the symbolism of his patient's dreams. He observes the connection of his imagery through a process that is called free association. In this, he allows or stimulates the patient to talk at random, saying everything that comes into his mind. The psychoanalyst listens, seeing connections that the patient does not. In good time all these things are put together and explained to the patient. The latter must come to realize what these hidden drives within him are, where they came from and where they lead him. The therapy is all within himself. The psychoanalyst makes it a point not to advise because by that he would be projecting his own aspirations and perhaps drives. Thus successful treatment depends entirely upon the co–operation of the patient and his ability to sort out these drives and to master them.

This is a brief and perhaps inadequate description, but it makes our point for us. In this form of therapy there can be no question of presenting motivation. It is an understanding of what is going on within one's self that is important at this stage. But we do not believe that therapy can remain at this level. Moreover, we are convinced that there are many other levels of human endeavor where conscious motivational therapy is required. Were we to accept the contrary to this, it would mean the abandonment of the whole position of voluntary self–control. If motivation is to be eliminated in all cases of difficulty in life on the grounds that we are responding only to unconscious drives, it would be the same as a denial of free will and the surrendering of all the Christian positions. Karl Stern writes: "One aspect of present–day psychiatry, and of psychoanalysis in particular, that evokes in many people a sense of apprehension and distrust, is the problem of guilt. It would almost seem as if the reality of good and evil, of innocence and culpability were being questioned with the advent of 'depth psychology.'"[9]

Therefore, in order to understand what is contained in the following pages, we wish to make it clear once and for all that we are not dealing precisely with the unconscious level, but with that level where the unconscious and the conscious meet. Within each of us there is the need to recognize and acknowledge the drives that lead us, and that may have been originally of an unconscious type but are now in some way within the reach of our consciousness. Self–analysis is one of the most valuable of man's activities. How often as we go through life do we need to stop and realize the true motives that have been leading us? "Know thyself" is still the key to wisdom. And it is to achieve greater knowledge in this field that we offer these few suggestions.

When the second Person of the Blessed Trinity assumed to Himself a human nature, He, by that divine act, sanctified the whole of human nature in all its aspects and relationships. The fullness of man lies, therefore, in realizing in its plenitude his incorporation in the Mystical Christ. This implies the full development of all his potentialities, even those that were primarily natural. The supernatural order does not destroy the natural but perfects it. So, in seeking the

---

[9]   Karl Stern, *The Third Revolution* (New York: Harcourt, Brace, 1954), p. 178.

fullness of Christ we will find also the fullness of man. And by the same token, by seeking the fullness of man, that is the legitimate work of the psychologist, we will not be led astray in our search for the fullness of Christ. On the contrary, the two roads lie parallel and with good will they can be made to meet where they should meet, at the center, in the heart of man and of God.

This is summed up in one of the prayers of the Holy Sacrifice of the Mass. "O God, who in creating human nature wonderfully dignified it, and even more wonderfully restored it, grant that ... we may become partakers of His Divine Nature who has deigned to share in our human nature." As in so many other things, the secret lies in what God Himself has done for us. Since God has deigned to become partaker of our human nature, He has ennobled it beyond our wildest hopes. What more legitimate pursuit, therefore, than to understand that nature in order that we may perfect it, and in understanding it also to understand and to participate more fully in the Divine Nature.

If in this matter we can make it clear to those who are not of the faith that we see no hostility in their work, that we, on the contrary, have the greatest admiration for the achievements of the human spirit in this magnificent field of research, we will be highly gratified. And we do firmly believe that there is no reason why the cross cannot be set upon psychology at the meeting of the ways, as King Alfred set the cross on Guthrum "at the parting of the ways."

> King Guthrum was a great lord,
> And higher than his gods —
> He put the popes to laughter,
> He chid the saints with rods.
>
> He took this hollow world of ours
> For a cup to hold his wine;
> In the parting of the woodways

There came to him a sign.

In Wessex in the forest,
In the breaking of the spears,
We set a sign on Guthrum
To blaze a thousand years.

Where the high saddles jostle
And the horse–tails toss,
There rose to the birds flying;
A roar of dead and dying;
In deafness and strong crying
We signed him with the cross.

Far out to the winding river
The blood ran down for days
When we put the cross on Guthrum
In the parting of the ways.[10]

---

[10] G. K. Chesterton, "Ballad of the White Horse," in *The Collected Poems of G. K. Chesterton* (London: Methuen, 1937), p. 302. Reprinted with permission of Methuen and Miss D. E. Collins.

CHAPTER 2

THE GOAL OF MATURITY

● ● ●

In all things human, self is the center of gravity of the universe.[11] For all who believe in Him, God is, of course, accepted as the objective center about which all revolves and upon which all depends. To put it philosophically, He is subsistent being itself (*ipsum esse subsistens*) and consequently the First Cause from which all else takes its being because all else is contingent, not having in itself the reason of its being. But this does not change the fact that He has created us in a world of self to which inevitably we refer all else. The fundamental psychological division of all things is that between self (ego)[12] and that which is not self (non–ego).

Psychologists have seized upon this important fact as a starting point for their teachings regarding human behavior. For example, they point out that practically all antisocial behavior is based not upon any inherent dislike for other humans or any innate inability to get along in society, but rather on some personal factor of maladjustment. Something is wrong in the ego; there is a lack of confidence,

---

[11] See C. S. Lewis, *Perelandra* (New York: Macmillan, 1943), p. 249.
[12] "By ego, I understand a complex of representations which constitute the centrum of my field of consciousness and appears to possess a very high degree of continuity and identity." C. G. Jung, *Psychological Types* (New York: Harcourt, Brace, 1944), p. 540.

frustration, or something similar that inspires distorted conduct toward others as a compensation or some other form of transfer.

Genesis of the Consciousness of Self

The child is born into the world completely unaware of self as a separate factor. His early impressions are the result of external stimuli, and it is some time before he becomes conscious that it is his ego that is receiving these impressions and making them meaningful. A clear indication of this is the tendency of the young child to refer to himself in the third person. He projects himself, as it were, and does not yet understand the fundamental difference between self and nonself.[13]

As a consequence, there can be no question at first of his dependence or independence. He is not conscious of self and hence does not realize that he must depend on all about him for his continued existence. A striking parallel is found in the lives of nations. When they are first founded as colonies they are not aware of a separate existence. They live for the mother country. A certain period must elapse before a distinct national identity arises to challenge that dependence and finally to cause the offspring to stand alone and to declare sovereignty and independence. And, if we may anticipate a question we will treat of later, this process is seldom, if ever, without friction.

Thus, the Creator places man at the very beginning of the path that he must tread. He begins completely dependent. He must become fully independent as a human person, fully self–developed in a very precise sense if he is to make a success of his existence.

---

[13]   This fact corresponds to the traditional teaching of the Schoolmen that "the human soul does not know itself directly but indirectly by 'reflection.'"

Self–Development—a Basic Need

Modern psychology is most insistent on this point. Man is a self–contained, self–governing agent. His destiny is to arrive at the full expression of his powers. If, somewhere along the line, he fails to achieve the proper development, if he is held by some chain of dependence that is not in accord with his nature as a free and sovereign agent, he will be stunted in growth, he will never reach the height of his power, and within himself he will feel the tension between what he is and what he should be.

The favorite example, and in fact the most recurring one in life, is that of the man (or woman) who has never developed sufficient confidence in himself and in his ability to meet life. This state of mind has received many names, most often that of "inferiority complex," although the term "inferiority feeling" is much more acceptable.[14] Here is a man who has not developed properly. He has not accepted himself, his powers, and his limitations. As a consequence happiness is impossible for him, and his whole life and effectiveness will be at least partly spoiled by this situation. He will refuse to accept the universe; he will become sour, embittered, jealous, asocial, or antisocial. He is a cog that does not fit in the machine and that will necessarily generate friction.

On the other hand, the well–adjusted man, not necessarily more talented, but better developed personally, will be relatively happy and contented, a useful citizen and a worthwhile relative and friend. What is the difference? One has developed to full maturity. He accepts himself as he is and in his relationship to others. The other, perhaps through factors of which he is entirely unconscious, has anxieties and insecurities to such a point that these dominate his

[14] See G. Geisel, *Personal Problems and Morals* (New York: Houghton Mifflin, 1943), sec. 16.

personality. He does not accept himself in the world as it is, with the resultant dislocation of his personality.

In a word, the complete development of self is the first goal of man and consequently his first preoccupation in the realm of psychological growth.

We have deliberately kept the discussion on a general level up to this point because in this manner we have been able to establish a basis that is unanimously accepted by psychologists, Christian or otherwise. But we must now further define the meaning of this development and its concomitant independence; in so doing we will have to distinguish between certain schools of psychological thought and leave some of the psychologists to follow their own road because we are convinced that they have, unfortunately, taken the wrong turn.

True Meaning of Self-Development

Self–development involves arriving at a maximum ability in the exercise of all our powers, but from a psychological point of view it means attaining the proper attitudes to self and to self–in–the–world. Given man's nature as a self–governing agent, this means self–assertion and independence. Some psychologists have pushed this subjective independence to an exaggerated degree. They have made of man the center of the universe, not only in the subjective and psychological sense but also objectively and ontologically. They have maintained that all internal subjection to other power is un-worthy of man and harmful to his psyche. God, then, is a link that must also be broken, a symbol of the parent link which must not remain dominant through life under pain[15] of continued immaturity and frustration.

---

[15] See D. Donnelly, *The Bone and the Star* (New York: Sheed and Ward, 1944), preface.

Such an attitude is, of course, unacceptable to us. The independence and self–assertion with which we are concerned is that which involves a legitimate breaking of all ties that would eventually stunt the growth of man and his attainment of full stature. We accept only the teaching of psychology that presents the dignity of man in terms of internal freedom from *undue* influences both from without and from within.

Parental authority, for example, is an excellent thing and during the years of his youth man must be dependent upon those who have given him life and who lead him to maturity. But the day must come when the full–grown person must stand, at least internally and as a person, upon his own feet. Continued psychological dominance by a parent has ruined many a life and particularly many a marriage. Here is a typical example from a psychological case history:

> Andrew J., an only child whose father died when An-
> drew was a young lad, became the chief object of the
> affections of a dominating and solicitous mother. In
> youth he gave evidence of fair ability, and in late adoles-
> cence he made some overtures towards establishing
> normal self–dependence. He enlisted during the Span-
> ish–American war, but was promptly brought home by
> his mother when he developed an illness. Later he mar-
> ried, but his wife soon affirmed that he must choose
> between her and his mother. He chose his mother, de-
> voted himself to satisfying her affections and whims,
> and received her motherly care in return. He never real-
> ized the promise of his youth in any vocational achieve-
> ment commensurate with his ability. He became and
> remained a subordinate clerk in a business office. When
> he was past fifty years of age, his mother died, and in a
> letter to a relative at that time he wrote: "I have nothing
> further to live for. I am just waiting to join mother."[16]

[16] Floyd L. Ruch, *Psychology and Life* (New York: Scott, Foresman, 1941), p. 580.

Proper independence or self–assertion is not an external thing. An invalid may be physically or economically dependent without in any way sacrificing his personal development. It is in the soul; it is the attribute of the unconquerable spirit of man. "My head is bloody but unbowed."[17] Consequently, it implies external freedom from exaggerated dependence upon some external factor and an internal freedom that makes a man master of himself, of his emotions, of his passions, of his fears, of unhealthy servitude to the opinions of others. In short, it signifies the full stature of the man who is the captain of his soul.

This is how an excellent spiritual writer of the present day expresses this age–old truth in terms of Christian mysticism:

> But then, if you care like this, you learn also not to care. If you learn to see God in all things, you will learn to love them according to His will, not your own self–will. If you see things as in eternity, you are less a prey to the pain of their passing, and so you can learn to be reverent and not proudly possessive. And where it is a question of legitimate possession and legitimate use and these are measured by the end that God has set for you, your manner of life and the work you do and the needs of your being—then you will learn more easily not to sin by excess or superfluity, nor to hold fast at all costs when God would take from you what He has given; you will learn more easily not to care.[18]

---

[17] Henley, William Ernest. "Invictus."
[18] Gerald Vann, O.P., *The Divine Pity* (New York: Sheed and Ward, 1946), p. 29. Reprinted with permission of Sheed and Ward.

CHAPTER 3

THE DISCOVERY OF SELF

● ● ●

Education and the Development of Self

The foregoing chapter has been a highly condensed presentation of the main principles of psychology governing the proper development of the ego. We will now consider some of the most important applications of these facts in the training of character. These applications are valid at any age but it is easier to see their scope in the forming of the young.

From what has been said it follows that one of the major preoccupations of the educator is to lead his charge toward self–realization. The very word education (*e–ducere*) connotes a drawing forth of the latent powers, a continued advance to a goal of achievement. In character formation, that goal is the establishing of the full human person in the sense defined above.

But this task is a delicate and difficult one. The youth must be led gently to take more and more responsibility, to act more and more for himself. The whole modern trend in education is inspired by the findings of psychology. Student government, the activity and the project theories, the emphasis on personal contribution in schoolwork, the emergence of the child, and the retirement of the teacher are all based upon the idea of developing self, of producing proper independence and self–assertion.

Every man must be taught his own worth. He must be treated with respect as a person. He must learn that his contribution to the world, however small, is important. He must judge himself by himself, not by comparison with others, because his worth is an absolute thing, not relative.

Such a spirit is bound to affect the personality and to bring us to an acceptance of self that will contribute immensely to our happiness. The worthwhile independence that accompanies this self–acceptance corresponds to a natural urge. We have pointed out the total dependence of the newborn infant. As the child advances he wishes to exercise his new–found powers. Observe the youngster of five or six when his mother wishes to take his hand to cross the street. Whereas a few months previous he gratefully accepted the outstretched hand, he now indignantly refuses it. He wishes to walk alone to convince the world, but most of all himself, that he is growing up, that he is becoming self–sufficient.

And what an interesting study it is to watch the developing personality of a child coupled with the assertion of self. The psychological processes are, particularly at first, much more connected with the physical than most suspect.

First there is the weaning by which the child becomes entirely independent of food of a direct mother–origin. This is followed by his first step. And even our language has recognition of this phase. To stand on one's feet has a psychological meaning recognized by all. The first ability to leave the hand of a sustaining adult has a deep repercussion in the soul of the child.

Then comes the first word. The Rev. D. H. Salman, O.P., an outstanding expert in animal psychology, outlined in a lecture to the Thomas More Institute for Adult Education (1957) the parallel growth of a human child and a chimpanzee. In the first stages there is little to choose between the rate of growth from any measurable viewpoint. However, at the precise moment when the child utters his first word the race is over. The child leaves his animal companion far behind.

This is standing on our own feet psychologically. The ability to express our thoughts gives us an independence, a sense of assurance that is incalculable.

From that moment the process of growth from the point of view of independence is almost entirely psychological. But it is still of the greatest importance. Just as the young child must learn to "stand on his own feet," "to speak his own mind," so some day must the young man and young woman learn to stand on their own feet and speak their own minds in the full sense of psychological maturity.

Psychology tells us that, if we wish to be mature in ourselves and influential with others, we must understand this urge. The most universal and most pained cry of youth is "We are being treated as children." They can forgive anything else, but not that. To treat them as younger than they are, or even as young as they are, strikes at the very roots of their self-esteem, at their cherished steps toward independence, the goal of their nature.

This attitude of youth, particularly of teenagers, has its parallel in the adult. He doesn't express it in the same way, but he always resents any violation of his ego. The average human being blossoms under the sun of the respect and of the confidence of others. That is why exaggerated paternalism of individuals or governments, however well meant, sooner or later arouse wrath and resentment. And the modern and fascinating study of mass psychology bears out that this is true also of groups and nations. Elections in democratic countries often show evidence of this phenomenon.

Leadership

All training in leadership is based on this concept. Leadership implies self–confidence, independent thinking, and the ability to act decisively. One does not possess these traits at birth, they must be developed, and only encouragement and the sharing of responsibility on the part of the elder generation can bring about sufficient self–confidence to produce leadership in the younger.

Dangers

The danger, of course, is that this spirit of independence will run wild.[19] The youth may come to despise the experienced advice of his elders. He may find such enjoyment in his own decisions that he will refuse further obedience even to legitimate authority. These are all pitfalls that beset the path of him who would guide the feet of youth. Some psychologists have been rather naïvely optimistic about how youth would respond to responsibility and self–assertion. A few years ago, guided by psychological considerations, many adults, parents, and others, subscribed to the principle of imposing the fewest possible restrictions on the young, to let them do mostly as they pleased. The resulting waves of delinquency that we experience to this day are at least a partial result of this exaggeration.

Assessing the Christian Position

The most conservative observer will readily admit that there is much good in the development of youth as outlined above. There is even a great deal upon which we might well examine our conscience. One of the greatest disabilities of some of our Catholic

---

[19] C. S. Lewis, *Perelandra,* chap. 16. The favorite and most convincing argument used by the Tempter against the Green Woman was that her God–given commandment was only in order to have her assert her independence.

school systems, and of some of our clergy–lay relationships, has been the failure to understand these urges of self–assertion and proper independence. We have made the mistake, not of loving too much, because true charity can suffer no excess, but of not disciplining our love sufficiently. We have been like proud and fond mothers who wish to do everything for their child and in the excess of their zeal do not permit the proper development that can only be attained by doing. In other words, we too have been and are sometimes over possessive when we are in authority.

Intellectually we have too often indulged in "spoon–feeding."[20] In the case of religious teachers, the children take the place of their own family. As a result, no effort is too great, no task too hard if it will help these "little ones." And so, in some cases, everything is done for the pupil. Formulas are prepared containing the maximum of truth in the minimum of words so that the children may have immediately at hand the answer to their problem. References are looked up and tabulated by the teacher to help the child along. Problems are worked out and difficulties avoided so as not to cause strain or worry.[21] Summaries to be learned by heart are the bankruptcy of any class or school or system. As was pointed out in a previous work, *The Catholic Public Schools of Quebec,*

[20] In the following remarks, that may sound unduly critical but that are meant only to help some of the most devoted people in the world or to suggest possibilities of bettering an already wonderful situation, we will speak mostly of our schools. But almost identical comment could be made regarding the attitude that sometimes exists in the clergy in regard to the adult faithful. They are, alas, frequently treated as children. Yet the same psychological principles apply here. Unless there is a feeling of mature participation — not of just being told — there will never be co–operation to the highest degree possible.

[21] In justice, however, it must be noted that this has not prevented the ascendancy of Catholic schools even in secular subjects.

In the schools of philosophy which dot the Catholic world there is a procedure which is difficult to justify in terms of this philosophy of education. It is what may be described as the "thesis technique." A philosophical subject is presented, and after a certain amount of definition (which is a good thing) the "thesis" is enunciated; for example: "The origin of living beings from non–living beings, or spontaneous generation, is unacceptable." Perhaps there isn't anything wrong with this in itself, but it is a very dangerous procedure. It is as though we were told: "Here is the thesis. The truth has been found for you. There is no need for you to look any further; simply understand what these other people have thought, and you will have wisdom." No such capsule learning ever led to wisdom. It is not sufficient to have the truth and then to learn the arguments which others have framed. The act of comprehension is the important thing, and it must always be an act of assimilation, an act of progressive understanding. The mind must contemplate the question at issue and make its own act of acceptance or rejection. And it must be led to do this, not commanded — not even in the name of truth.

How much more effective was the technique of Thomas Aquinas, who began almost daringly by challenging the opposition, marshalling in first place their best arguments on the subject under discussion, which was always proposed as a question, never as a statement. After he had presented the best that the opposition had to offer, he would then arrive at the expression of his own opinion and what his own insight had brought to mind on the subject. Only at this point would he turn again to the arguments of the opposition and show where they had erred. What a pity that the educational philosophy and technique of this great master were not fully carried out in many of our schools! And what is said of the teaching of philosophy in some Catholic schools may also be said of the teaching of almost any subject in almost any school. It is a great temptation for the master to take what he has learned, to reduce it to a capsule, and to think that it can be assimilated like a pill. It is in a sense the easy way, but again it is the mistaken idea that one generation can do the work for another.[22]

It should not be necessary to point out that we are speaking of extreme cases and that this is far from being true of all Catholic systems and particularly of all religious. We are pointing rather to a trend and a danger that has too often been realized in fact, rather than making a sweeping generalization that would be as unjust as it would be false. Besides, no one has greater respect and admiration for religious teachers and their work, but it remains true that this excess does exist and this temptation to an excessive concept of zeal is ever present to us. As a result, we have sometimes failed to make our students intellectually independent and capable of conducting their own research.

In character formation the same danger exists and the same fault has been prevalent although, of course, it is much harder to register the results. Failure here does not mean flunking out in a university course. It means flunking out in life with perhaps the loss of an immortal soul. Student government has been exaggerated in some circles, but in many Catholic schools the absence of student participation, the refusal to grant student responsibility, has been even more exaggerated.

[22] G. Emmett Carter, *The Catholic Public Schools of Quebec* (Toronto: Gage, 1957), pp. 104–105.

Again, the cause may have been the overwhelming desire to help, but in looking at the results one is reminded of the ironical prayer of the man who said: "Protect me from my friends, O Lord; I can take care of my enemies myself."

There have been, and are, schools where the attitude of those in authority may be summed up as follows: "It is understood that you are going to sin as soon as you get the opportunity; consequently we are going to do everything in our power to give you no opportunity." And then the battle of wits is on. A supervision or spy system on one hand matches its ingenuity with the students on the other. The outcome is not hard to predict. Even if the authorities could win while youth is in school, what kind of a preparation for life would this be? Virtue is from within, not from without. Unless we are brought to accept our own responsibilities before God and man, there can be no question of character or strength of will. If we convince our subordinates that we have no confidence in them, that they will fall as soon as the occasion arises, we may be sure that they will have no confidence in themselves and will in fact do what is so clearly expected of them.

Apart from this extraordinarily inept and unpsychological approach, that is predominantly negative, fortunately becoming less and less prevalent, there is the refusal to give others positive responsibility in their own tasks.

We have seen the need of bringing the child to maturity by having him do for himself. He must come to an esteem of himself and a confidence in his powers, and this can be attained only by actual exercise of his powers. The same is true of adult participation. If there is a church activity, a concert to be staged, an excursion to be planned, why should not those participating take most of the responsibility? The good done in building up the ego, by the feeling of belonging, is immeasurable. Errors will be made, of course. But errors in matters like this may even be beneficial in a way. They are at least the proof that the young or the lay are doing things by themselves. It is assumed that the faculty or the clergy could do better, but it is not the faculty that is being educated or the clergy who must be drawn in. We wonder what would happen if we took the same attitude in physical development as we too often do in Church or in intellectual or moral problems. What would we think of a program in sports or athletics that called exclusively for the periodic appearance of trained athletes who perform for the benefit of the student body? Would we expect to develop muscle and sinew in this manner? Would we hope to win athletic championships through the skill of students who had never tried for themselves? But when it comes to preparing a speech in honor of the parish priest, the student usually sees it in time to memorize it and then proceeds to deliver an agglomeration of sentiment that no student would ever have conceived and that betrays in the first sentence the identity of its author. And why is it that the lay advisers of the clergy have the international reputation of being yes–men?

Psychological Reason for Failure

Besides the reasons given above for this tendency in Catholic circles to avoid conferring responsibility, there is another and deeper one, at least in our opinion.

To give responsibility means to relinquish authority to some degree. Authority in Catholic circles is for the most part in the hands of religious (priests, brothers, nuns). Religious are uniformly dedicated to a life of chastity. Now there are three fundamental human drives:[23] (*a*) the preservation of self, (*b*) the propagation of the species, (*c*) the will to power. Celibacy involves the repression of the second of these.

---

[23] See W. F. Cunningham, *Pivotal Problems of Education* (New York: Macmillan, 1940).

What is more natural than to expect that this repression will take the form of a transfer of drive at least in some degree and that the will to power will be proportionately strengthened?

Besides, parenthood is the normal means of satisfaction for the drive to power. Since this is impossible for the celibate, he tends to concentrate on the power given him by his position. Religious are notoriously jealous of their rights, privileges, and prerogatives. We have only to apply this principle to the governing of others to understand why it is so difficult to bring some religious to grant responsibility and consequently a share in their authority.

It might be answered in rebuttal to this that perhaps what we have called a weakness is in reality a strength. Perhaps the divergence between the teaching of psychology and the practice of some Catholic circles indicates simply that the psychologists are wrong and not in conformity with Christian principles, and that brings us to the main point.

Catholic Teaching and Psychological Findings

Not only are the findings of psychology, as described above, in conformity with Christian asceticism, but the moral principles laid down by Christ and developed by the Church are the most effective and the only sure way of attaining the results desired.

The goal is the proper development of the ego, self–assertion, legitimate independence. As a goal this is in complete accord with Christian teaching. In fact, as we have said, it is only in the light of our faith that the end can be clearly visualized.

In the divine plan every individual has a vocation, a destiny to fulfill, a role to play that is unique and incommunicable.[24] This is

---

[24] See H. Schumacher, *Social Message of the New Testament* (Milwaukee: Bruce Publishing Company, 1937).

and always has been the teaching of Christianity. In fact, only in Christianity is the concept of the absoluteness of the human person respected. The doctrine of the Mystical Body clearly demonstrates the idea that each of us has a role to play that can never be accomplished by anyone else. God has deigned to associate us with the work of Redemption. It is a duty personal to each of us to "make up in our flesh the things that are wanting to the sufferings of Christ."[25] And what can be wanting to that infinite merit except our participation and co–operation?

All the human reasoning in the world, all the demonstrations of the most able psychologists remaining on a purely natural level are not capable of establishing a truly adequate reason why life is worthwhile, why a person with a physical disability need not grieve, why the untalented are just as important as the talented. There is only one reason why the human person is important and that is because he is in possession of an immortal soul that is destined for eternal happiness in God.

Our personalities will never be fully developed on this earth. Only under the brilliance of the Light of Glory will our intellects open up to the fullness of truth and our wills encompass the plenitude of good. This is the real destiny and the complete fulfillment of every human personality. That is why the disabilities, the failures, the inferiorities of this life are not overwhelmingly important. That is the only reason why all may be happy whatever their human lot. And what a weapon that is for the psychologist! What a guarantee against discouragement, feelings of inferiority, dissatisfaction, refusal to accept the universe and all the other things that fundamentally prevent man from accepting himself and developing his ego in conformity with the circumstances of his life!

[25] Col. 1:24.

One of the best proofs of this contention may be found in the attitude toward persons and individuals that becomes prevalent whenever the Christian spirit dies out of a given State or group. The absolute value of the human person is then lost sight of. His incommunicability is no longer accepted. Nor could it be, because he is no longer an absolute but a function. He is judged in relation to his abilities or his contribution to the State, or whatever happens to be the ruling deity. Respect for human dignity inevitably disappears. Man is no longer a person but a number and a function registered on a card–index file. He has so much physical strength, or beauty, he has so much intellect or skill and so forth. If he ceases to be useful, the logical conclusion is euthanasia, or any of the other un–Christian practices that arise under these conditions.[26] And this is only the reflection of the general attitude that must prevail. The whole scale of values of such a society deals with relative things such as "beauty, brains, and brawn," making it obviously impossible to inspire anything but arrogance in those who "have" and discouragement in those who "have not."

Our own civilization, inasmuch as it has not become Christian, or has ceased to be, reflects this false scale of human values with the resultant psychological disasters. A suicide is always a psychological disaster. It always means that some poor soul has died in ignorance of the true value within him, that he has accepted a false scale of value as the ultimate.

If it were not so tragic it would be amusing to see the purely materialistic psychologists contradict themselves. They try to build up the

[26] See *Moscow 1979* by Eric and Christine von Kuhnelt–Leddihn (New York: Sheed and Ward, 1954). The fate of the no–longer–useful is the "utilization factory" where their skins are made into brief cases, their teeth into ivory products, etc. This is the logical outcome of the God–State system.

human personality, the value of the ego, and with one metaphysical principle they destroy the only possible basis for human value, the immortal soul. They champion the cause of the little and the weak and the discouraged; they tell them to cheer up, that life is worthwhile, that there is value in every human ego and a contribution to be made, but they pass by in silence or openly sneer at a Figure who sits on a mountainside and patiently explains: Blessed are the poor, the meek, the persecuted, the just, the clean of heart, the peacemakers, *because* they shall possess the Kingdom of Heaven. And that kingdom, He has said, is within us. It begins in our souls and leads us on to the knowledge and love of God. And *that* is why life is worthwhile whatever the conditions. This is applied psychology the like of which the world had never seen and that it has never since approached.

Nor is it only in the question of the end or the goal of life that Christianity pushes the findings of psychology to their logical and sole possible conclusion. In the means to the end, that is, in the conduct of life itself, it is only Christian teaching that can give the full and final answer.

Psychology says that you must grow to your full stature, you must develop your ego, you must be an independent adult. Satisfaction, proper adjustment, a full and happy life are only for him who learns to take himself as he is, to accept his inabilities and develop his abilities. We might sum up all their teaching in the popular phrase, "Be yourself." In this phrase we have everything. Each one of us has a certain store of abilities and opportunities; self–assertion means to make the best of them and to find in maturity the fullness of ourselves. Each one of us has to battle with forces within and without which would enslave us and keep us psychologically children. "Be yourself" means to accept our adulthood and our responsibilities, to play out our role because no one else can play it for us. So speaks psychology.

Humility

That she speaks well, no one can deny. But it is equally undeniable that only Christian principles can furnish the complete solution to her teaching. There is a great Christian virtue that we will dare to call the great psychological virtue. It is our firm conviction that this virtue properly explained and *inculcated* into the lives of men, preferably at the plastic time of their youth, is the answer to the whole teaching of psychology of self–assertion and adjustment. We refer to the "unknown" virtue of humility.

Undoubtedly it sounds like a paradox to speak of self–assertion and humility in the same breath. But have we not consistently summed up the teachings of psychology in the axiom "Be yourself." And what else is humility? "Humility," says the great St. Teresa, "is truth." Let us then look at ourselves and see what the truth is and if in fact "the truth will make us free."[27]

"We are worthwhile. Convince yourself of your own value," says the psychologist. "Whatever you are you are the only one of your particular individuality. You must realize that you have something to contribute. That is why you must be properly independent, free, mature."

And what has humility to do with all this? Humility is the virtue that consistently teaches us our own worthlessness, impresses upon us our nothingness, our dependence, not the contrary. Such has always been the prevalent and universal teaching to youth. But there is another side of the truth that is humility, a side that Christian educators have too often passed over in silence. It has been an unfortunate silence, because the psychologists are right in saying that a sense of insecurity and inferiority can be disastrous. Remember we have said that the truth of psychology can force us to look more

---

[27] John 8:32.

closely at our Christian teaching and perhaps to see things we have not seen, or at any rate to bring them to wider use.

But how can humility speak of worth? It is unheard of! Indeed? Then let us, too, hasten across the mountainous region of Judea to the tiny village of Ain Karem—and as we go let us roll back the years. Two thousand of them. We hear a song of joy that has echoed down the ages, and it comes from a human being, a being of flesh and blood, of Adam's stock. And what is the song? "My soul doth magnify the Lord ... because He hath done great things to me ... He hath exalted the humble ... and behold from henceforth all generations shall call me blessed."[28]

Who is it that dares to speak so? A royal king? A great genius, a conquering general? Not at all. It is a young girl of not more than fourteen or fifteen years, a girl from a tiny Jewish town, of a despised and conquered race on the uttermost confines of the Roman Empire. Is she lacking in humility? The Fathers have maintained that it was her humility in particular that drew God down into her virginal womb. "Behold the handmaid of the Lord." Not only was she the most humble of God's creatures, but in recognizing her own greatness in this manner she was doing something entirely consonant with the virtue of humility.

The Psychological Effect of True Humility

Humility, then, is truth. By its exercise we take the proper attitude to ourselves and the universe. We can "be ourselves" to the utmost. Frustration, insecurity, feelings of inferiority are impossible to the humble man.[29] In its well-known function humility teaches us that

---

[28] Luke 1:46–48.

[29] At any rate on a conscious level. There is a deep problem of neurosis that is not imputable as moral guilt in any way. Can the neurotic also be humble? We submit that he can by consciously accepting his neurosis

we are nothing. We were created, that is, made out of nothing. We are kept in existence by a continuous act of God's creative will. We were born in sin and we have added to that by our personal sins. Apart from our actual guilt there is in us the possibility of an evil so deep and perverted that we could be worse than the worst the world has ever known.

Intellectually we are blind, leaders of the blind. The reaches of natural knowledge alone are far beyond our ken. A man who becomes proficient in one tiny branch of knowledge is hailed as a genius. Yet what does he know? And beyond lies the rest of the universe—unknown and unexplored by us. And beyond that, unattainable, lies God. What is man but a shadow?

Physically we are miniscule. A breath of air, a stone, a tiny piece of lead, a microscopic germ—any of these things is sufficient to bring us to death and dissolution.

Is there anything psychologically comforting in this? A great deal. In dealing with our relationships to others we will see that the realization of our common lot is a great comfort. It is said that "misery loves company," and that apparently ignoble attitude comes from a deep psychological need. Once we recognize that our nature is weak and that error and frailty are our natural inheritance, we cease to be surprised and discouraged at it. Of course, for those who believe only in nature, there is reason for discouragement, and it is here that the psychologist who goes no further is defeated.

But if in conjunction with this darkness of ignorance and weakness of will we consider our true greatness, we have reason to rejoice, we have something to live for, we have an incentive to develop our ego, our abilities, our personalities. We too can sing, "He hath done

inasmuch as it is beyond his control as a disability willed by God and not basically different from any other type of illness or suffering.

great things to me." We look within and what do we find? "You are a chosen generation, a kingly priesthood."[30] "And to all who received him, he gave the power to be the sons of God."[31] We have been raised to the supernatural order. Our destiny is to share for all eternity the very life of the Blessed Trinity. Already within us, if we will, is this divine life, growing with us. We are members of Christ, eternally important in helping to save our brethren; we are, in a sense, coredeemers. Our every action is important—eternally so.

And to whom is this possible? To those who have beauty, brain, brawn? Do we need political influence or great wealth? We have only to will it. The smallest can be the greatest. "God wishes all men to be saved and to come to the knowledge of the truth."[32] There is absolutely no reason for conscious frustration. "Be yourself" means to accept your position as God's creature and at the same time to accept in your outstretched hands the bounty of your Creator. His gifts are not external like the favors of earthly kings, but gifts that make *us* great. "All generations shall call *me* blessed."

What an impact such teaching is bound to have on the lives of the young. Accept yourself as you are. You have not a facile memory, you have not a nimble brain, your eyes are crooked, or your leg is lame. You are not able to run with the others or study with the others. Your parents are poor and your clothes are shabby. What of it? *You* are great. And you are great because God has made you so. "You are the sons of God and heirs to the kingdom of heaven."[33] From all eternity God chose you to be upon the earth, to make your contribution to His glory and to the salvation of your fellow men. Whatever your position, you alone can do it. You are tremendously

---

[30] 1 Pet. 2:9.
[31] John 1:12.
[32] 1 Tim. 2:4.
[33] Rom. 8:17.

important—to God. Here psychology and the Cross meet and go hand in hand.

And the stage is set to answer the question as to why we must give legitimate independence and participation to others.

CHAPTER 4

INDEPENDENCE WITHOUT REBELLION

● ● ●

The question of independence in youth finds its solution in this same supernatural humility.[34]

We have already pointed out two dangers in the training of youth. The first is not to allow youth sufficient independence, to repress all self–assertion, to restrain and subordinate in an exaggerated manner. The psychological result is either immaturity with its resultant frustrations or rebellion and antisocial attitudes. In any case, the young man or woman is not led to stand on his own feet and is not equipped to deal with the eventualities of life as a properly independent, self–sufficient adult.

The other extreme, into which non–Christian psychologists and educators fall most often, is that of encouraging independence and self–assertion in a manner detrimental to proper obedience and to legitimate authority. The reason why such individuals fail in this way is that their findings lack the balancing force of Christian revelation. The total and supernatural view of man that is included in Christian humility means the acceptance of the whole truth about man. And part of that whole truth is Original Sin and its effects upon the human race. To try to build a course of conduct for men without

---

[34] Supernatural humility presupposes the virtue of faith, because faith is the door to the supernatural.

recognition of that all–influencing factor is to doom one's efforts to certain failure. Many modern psychologists are still consciously or unconsciously the disciples of Rousseau and maintain that all man needs for happiness is to be unchecked and uninhibited.[35]

Christian Viewpoint

Christian humility steers its course between the shoals. Man is a member of a fallen race; he has lost the preternatural gifts of his first parents: freedom from ignorance and concupiscence and death. His lower nature may rebel against his higher and he may rebel against his God and the universe. In fact, one of the most interesting psychological studies is that of the genesis and development of rebellion in man. In following our description of it, notice that the starting point and guiding spirit throughout is pride, the vice opposed to humility.

The Origin of Rebellion

Man in the state of innocence was incapable of the lower forms of rebellion, as was probably the whole universe. He was free of lust or greed because his lower faculties were subject by divine decree to his intellect. In turn, his intellect had special light and knowledge whereby man always sought his proper end, even in seeking to achieve the aims of his so–called lower nature. There was only one possibility of sin and that was in the spiritual faculties. This possibility existed because God had chosen to leave man free and to put him through a test so that his love and service would be given freely and finally rewarded by the Beatific Vision. Once man had attained this vision, he would have final and complete impeccability in the splendor of Truth and the irresistible attraction of the Good that is God.

---

[35] See J. F. Brown, *The Psychodynamics of Abnormal Behavior* (New York: McGraw–Hill, 1940), p. 240.

Satan then struck through that single possibility of sin. Writers and preachers and teachers have sometimes portrayed the sin of Adam and Eve as a sin of lust or of greed for food or something else of that nature. This is impossible in the light of what we have seen and also in the light of the satanic temptation: "You shall be as Gods, knowing good and evil."[36] Indeed the approach is masterly. The serpent of Genesis does not offend the sensibilities or the loyalties of Eve by a direct statement of fact. He begins much more subtly by a question: "Why hath God commanded you?" He makes his victim wonder about the wisdom, the fairness of the divine prescription and only then follows it up with a suggestion—could it possibly be that God is forbidding this because you might become His equal if you took this road? And now the stage is set. The appeal to pride is obvious. Then follows the first rebellion, the first manifestation of improper independence in the world. Man *rebels in his mind* against God. This begins the whole series of rebellions. Because of this primary dislocation the whole organization of submission goes wrong. The lower faculties rebel. Man now "does not the things that he wills but the things he wills not, those he does." He sees "the law of his members fighting against the law of his mind."[37]

Another rebellion follows immediately. The natural universe in turn is freed from the dominion of him who wished to be freed from the dominion of God and the elements run their own course. The animals no longer obey the rebellious one, nor do the winds and the weather. It is the price of pride.

Psychological Effect of Rebellion in the Individual

Within man himself it is the beginning of neuroses and psychoses. The unbalancing makes itself felt almost immediately.

[36] Gen. 3:1.
[37] See Rom. 7:19, 23.

What did Adam do immediately after the sin? He blamed the whole thing on Eve. Psychologists call it "transfer of blame." We see it re–enacted all around us because of fear, insecurity, maladjustment in general. Why did Cain kill Abel? Because he was jealous, suffering from a psychological malady. Some psychiatrists may not admit it, but they owe their profession to Adam and Original Sin.

Rebellion in Society

Nor is the process of rebellion limited to the individual. Society has had to suffer the same effects on all its levels. To illustrate this we can give one example of the same causal factors at work in a rebellion leveled against the authority of Church and State. Many unbiased historians today admit that the Protestant rebellion was not heretical in its cause. Heresy was introduced to stabilize a condition of affairs that was first brought about by *pride,* by greed for Church possessions, and to some degree by lust. In other words, it wasn't just an attack upon tyrannical and illegitimate authority but a true rejection of religious authority because it stood in the way of designs that were evil, at least in part. Rebellion began here against religious authority, the Church. But see how quickly it spread, because all authority is one in the final analysis. Thus when Elizabeth in England lay dying after completing the break with religious authority, the generation was already born that would send the king's head toppling too.

And the present–day decline in family authority is the direct result of the spread of this rebellion to the level of the family. Totalitarianism has completed the process of standing the world on its head, by denying God and enslaving the individual who began the process so that he might be greater and is now in danger of being reduced to so little.

Christian Via Media

Man, then, has inherited the tendencies to pride and to self–indulgence. In his youth he must be taught self–discipline both within, in his own nature and the use of his faculties, and without, in his submission to God and all legitimate authority that by definition is of God.

Such is part of the true picture of man that he must accept if he is not to imitate the pride of the angels who would not serve, or the pride of his first parents who wanted to be something they were not, "like God." Self–discipline tempers the search after independence without destroying it and channels the drive for self–assertion and mature independence because it leads man to accept his greatness and his destiny solely because of their true source and real origin—from the gift of God, not from self or from man's intrinsic worth. "He gave them power to be made the sons of God, to them that believe in his name. Who are born not of blood, nor of the will of the flesh, nor of the will of man, but of God."[38] Far from lessening a man's worth or making him feel inferior, this attitude is indispensable in any search for true human greatness. Fr. Farrell has explained this relationship as follows:

> One of the early calumnies against the Christian religion, that it was a religion of slaves and weaklings, was due as much to this emphasis on humility as it was to the historical character of the early converts. Yet Christ did not come to make men slaves, to send them groveling in the dust; His own summation of His mission was that men "might have life and have it more abundantly," that their "joy might be full." Nor did the early Christians misunderstand His aims when they insisted on humility, for one of the explicit lessons He gave was "learn of me, for I am meek and

[38] John 1:12–13.

humble of heart." The question is not so much a matter of attempting reconciliation between irreconcilables—the subjection of humility and the full, joyous abundance of life; it is rather a matter of understanding that one cannot be had without the other. Humility, as a matter of fact, places the very first condition of progress towards a full life, the condition of subjection. Showing a man his limitations, keeping his hopes within the bounds of his abilities, humility keeps a man in his proper place; and this not in a particular respect, but universally. Consequently it cuts out at the roots the great obstacles to happiness, the obstacles that consist in putting ourselves above all others, in seeking our own excellence, caught up as a sleepwalker by his dream to wander blindly out of our proper world. That obstacle goes by the name of pride.[39]

Such, if only all psychologists could see it, is the continuation and the consummation of that primeval struggle. The first man would not accept his own littleness, his role as a creature. He wanted to be like God. He did not have humility, and it led him and all his children to disaster. As we have pointed out, he rapidly exhibited signs of psychological maladjustment. He indulged in "transfer of blame" to his wife—who went right along the same path and blamed the serpent. He feared and disobeyed. Hiding from the voice of God, he rationalized that fear by advancing his state of nakedness. His first son became so maladjusted that jealousy drove him to kill his brother Abel, the guiltless one. Fallen man, in his refusal of humility, is well on the way in his story of guilt, unhappiness, and all the manifestations of psychological upset and dislocation.

[39] Walter Farrell, *A Companion to the Summa* (New York: Sheed & Ward, 1945), Vol. 3, pp. 463–464.

On the other hand the humble man of faith, in and through the First–Born of God, actually achieves what Adam sought but sought badly. He becomes a son of God. Men of faith are "sons of God" and "partakers of the divine nature."[40] Christian humility confers all the fruits of perfect adjustment to our status and nature. "The fruit of the Spirit is charity, joy, peace, patience, benignity, goodness, longanimity, mildness, faith, modesty, continency, chastity. Against such there is no law."[41] "Lord, to whom shall we go? thou hast the words of eternal life."[42] Yes, and of a well–adjusted life here below.

Responsibility of Education

"The wrath of God is revealed from heaven against … those that detain the truth of God in injustice."[43] The responsibility that falls to the Christian is a terrifying one. He holds in his hands the answers to the problems of youth. He is pledged to use all the natural means that psychology prescribes, supernaturalizing them by putting them through the purification of Christian principles and revealed truth.

In this question of the development of self that has so far predominantly occupied our attention, Christian teaching has always been basically psychological in scope, even though, as we have said, the practice of some schools has at times been unsound and unpsychological and consequently not truly Christian.

Perhaps the best way to describe how the application of these principles should be attained is to refer briefly to one of the phases of Christian living in which the greatest comprehension of psychology has been in evidence. We mean that awakened sense of universal dynamism in the Church that has been called Catholic Action.

[40] John 1:12; 2 Pet. 1:4.
[41] Gal. 5:22–24.
[42] John 6:69.
[43] Rom. 1:18.

The Psychological Contribution of Catholic Action

We have already alluded to the sense of responsibility and worthwhileness that comes to us when we realize what it really means to be a member of the Mystical Body. Through the great goodness of God, man is greater in the redemptive economy than he would have been in the state of innocence without incorporation in Christ.[44] We are coredeemers, sharing in the priesthood and the victimhood of Christ and "fill up those things that are wanting in the suffering of Christ, in my flesh."[45] This doctrine was realized in high degree by the early Christians and we find it in full view in the writings of the Churchmen of the Middle Ages. With the Reformation, heresy forced the emphasis from the middle path, and it was taught that all men were priests (which rapidly meant that no men were priests), that the Redemption of Christ could not be lacking and so we had only to cover ourselves with His merits, and that it was fantastic to teach that we ourselves did anything to further our redemption.

The psychological effect of such teaching is obvious. I am not interested in what I do not share. If I am a spectator at the Redemption well and good, but do not be surprised if I am bored and begin to look around for something I can do myself. The decrease in religious practice among the people infected with the heresy inevitably bore out what a good psychologist could have predicted.

Nor did the counterattack of orthodoxy save us from some unhappy results in the practical order. Obliged to defend the priesthood, the hierarchy of authority, and the very structure of the Church itself with its foundation on Peter, the theologians fulminated against the pretensions of the laity. Within the Church the pendulum swung

---

[44] See G. Ellard, *Christian Life and Worship,* rev. ed. (Milwaukee: Bruce Publishing, 1956), Chaps. 1, 2, 3.

[45] Col. 1:24.

in the opposite direction, but too far. "Keep the laity in their place. They are not priests, they have not received Orders, they are not a part of the governing Hierarchy." All true, but the insistence on this side of the doctrine produced some results similar to the heresy of denying the priesthood and the operation of the Mystical Body.

The priesthood kept its place and its understanding of its fundamental role of working per *Ipsum et cum Ipso et in Ipso* for the salvation of the world, but the laity felt out of the picture. The *laissez-faire* attitude "let the clergy do it" became prevalent. The idea that the Church and the hierarchy are synonymous and that the laity are a kind of inert mass to be pushed and kicked or flattered and cajoled through the Pearly Gates took hold of the minds of Catholic people everywhere. Such terminology as "hearing Mass" betrayed the general mentality.

Our Holy Father Pope Pius XI was not the first of recent pontiffs to point out the danger, but it was he who coined the phrase "Catholic Action" to express the proper perspective and who launched the crusade that promises to re–establish the laity in full possession of their Christian prerogatives and in the understanding of their redemptive role.[46]

So much has been said on Catholic Action and so much has been excellently written on the psychology of the movement that we will not develop the theme.

---

[46] Fr. Morlion, O.P., holds the opinion that only the laity can save the Church from relative disaster in the present cycle of its history. He maintains that the Church is in the third period of its development, each of the first two periods corresponding roughly to a thousand years. In the first period it was the time of establishment and organization in which the founding of dioceses and parishes predominated. The second period had the religious orders most in evidence. The third or present period is the hour for the laity to make their definite contribution.

See also the excellent works of Fr. Yves Congar, O.P., *Lay People in the Church* (London: Bloomsbury, 1957), and of Henri de Lubac, S.J., *Catholicism* (London: Burns, Oates, 1950).

It is, however, very much to our point to say that Catholic Action offers perhaps the best and most fertile field for developing a sure, balanced, Christian maturity. We may now take it as established that the Christian view of man is the only sure way to proper self–assurance and legitimate, balanced independence. By the same token Catholic Action is the road to the total and thorough realization of the Christian view through intimate, individual, and personalized participation in the Redemption.

The essence of the movement is to make the laity operative in the Mystical Body. In the light of the psychological principles stated above, this means, immediately, the conferring of responsibility, of independent actions, the involving of the principle of interest, and all the other things that are required to develop self–assertion and mature adulthood.

In the most worthwhile cause man could dream of, each individual becomes in Catholic Action a person of great importance. He understands that his action will result in the salvation of souls. And in the carrying out of the movement, if it is done as it should be, the layman acts under the hierarchy but by himself. Religion is no longer a set of formulas, an insurance against fire of the eternal variety, but a living, pulsing interest. His brethren need him, the Church needs him, Christ Himself needs him. He must act on his fellows, he must plan, he must take responsibility, he must be mature. Catholic Action can save the world. It will also do much to develop proper self–assurance and adjustment.

CHAPTER 5

OVERCOMING THE DIFFICULTIES

● ● ●

The term "compensation" means that nature, to meet emergency situations, draws from its resources powers that are sometimes hidden. A blind man, for instance, does not possess any stronger sense of touch than does a man with sight, but he "compensates" for his loss of one faculty by developing another. The adrenalin that is pumped into the blood stream during high emotional tension enables us to meet emergency situations that normally would overcome us. Thus, Ruch[47] cites the case of a man who dashed into his burning office and threw out of the window a small safe containing valuable papers. After the fire he found he was unable to lift the safe once the emotion of the moment had passed.

Compensation in the psychological sphere is very similar to such physiological compensation. It consists in finding and accepting an equivalent value as a substitute for some form of achievement that is denied us by force of circumstances usually beyond our control.[48]

The functioning of compensation can be beneficial or harmful. Glen Cunningham, famous racing star, was physically weak in youth;

[47] See Floyd L. Ruch, *Psychology and Life* (New York: Scott, Foresman, 1937), p. 186.
[48] See Rudolf Allers, *Psychology of Character* (New York: Sheed and Ward, 1935), p. 93.

59

Demosthenes had a speech defect. Many a handicapped man or woman through an effort of the will has profited by opportunities afforded by the very handicap itself. Helen Keller is an outstanding modern example, as was President Franklin D. Roosevelt.

But on the other hand, there can be great danger when the effort to compensate takes unorthodox channels. The drunkard who has tried to drown his sorrow in alcohol is a well–known figure in both life and literature. In children it is not an exaggeration to say that the great majority of cases of delinquency or of habitual misconduct have something of compensation in them.

Education has often failed to realize this fact, summed up by the dictum of Fr. Flanagan that there is no such thing as a bad boy. Something has thrown the youngster off the track. A feeling of physical inferiority may cause moral misbehavior because the afflicted individual takes this means to impose his personality on those about him. This is illustrated most effectively by Shakespeare's portrayal of Richard III.

Emotional, intellectual, or scholastic difficulties have started more "bad boys" (or girls) on their way than the average teacher dreams of. Most educators take the attitude that so–and–so is inferior academically because he misbehaves, because he is mischievous or lazy. Yet very often it is just the other way around. He is lazy, mischievous, and misbehaves because he is inferior academically. Somewhere he failed to make the grade, perhaps only in one subject. From difficulty he went to discouragement. Then, to cover up his deficiency, he pretends sophistication, boredom. He scoffs at the "plugger," "the teacher's pet." He begins to attract the attention he so greatly desires by acts of bravado, misbehavior in class, and perhaps, finally, lawlessness. He is compensating.

All through life and in every phase of it, every mental state may be the effect of compensation or may be affected by it. It is intimately connected with the tendency to community because it is usually caused by the human desire for social approval or attention of one kind or another.

Psychologists have presented many and varied directives to show the path of proper compensation to the young. Most of their motives are, however, purely natural. They point out the success of people who have overcome initial obstacles; they argue on the worthwhileness of "success" and the value of effort. But once a young person has become discouraged, once his basic security has been affected by failure of one kind or another, either real or imagined, the remedy must be applied to the very evil itself. In some cases the presentation of future achievement may succeed, but generally it will not. On the motivation level only the Christian concept of value and the Christian presentation of man's true role in the world can cure the wound.

St. Paul has spoken of the "momentary and light of our tribulation."[49] This must be interpreted carefully. It serves no purpose to pretend that some types of handicaps or difficulty are not a grievous burden. The child with the lame leg or the crooked eye, the orphan and the dispossessed, the dull and the untalented have an unanswerable reply: "It is all very well for *you* to talk, you don't have to suffer what I have."

The only procedure is to present the good in the difficulty, a good that may be entirely supernatural. There is often no consolation in a situation except the knowledge that God wishes it and that we may in this manner join our sufferings with those of Christ and thus be victims with Him in the work of redemption. We "fill up those things that are wanting to the sufferings of Christ, in [our] flesh."[50] Even when we ourselves are to blame, there is no reason for discouragement because "to them that love God, all things work

49 2 Cor. 4:17.
50 Col. 1:24.

together unto good,"[51] and St. Augustine points out in what sense this includes even sin.

The line of compensation is then clearly indicated. The value of the person, his place before God, a wise and kindly Providence that has foreseen all eventualities and planned them for his greater good—these considerations form the background for his hope and encouragement. The love God has for him, a love shared by all worthy of the name of Christian, a love that has as its object not the externals of his life but his priceless soul and irreplaceable personality—these are the levers upon which he can raise himself to feel that he belongs, that his is not an insuperable obstacle, and that he will find kindness and help and understanding.

Then if he is fortunate enough to find a kind, wise person, a teacher or elder for the young, a friend for the not–so–young, who will put in his way opportunities for little successes, praising him for them and for his least effort, he will come to taste the sweetness of real approval. He will leave the cheap imitation of achievement he has been seeking in his daydreaming or in his "adventures" outside the law to gain the attention and admiration he thought impossible in the paths of truth and goodness.

[51] Rom. 8:28.

SECTION TWO

THE OUTGOING SELF

CHAPTER 6

PSYCHOLOGY'S "COMMUNITY"
AND CHRISTIAN SOLIDARITY

● ● ●

We have already indicated that the ego and the non–ego constitute the fundamental division of being from a psychological point of view. Though distinct, the ego and non–ego are not isolated. Proper or improper internal adjustment of the ego is bound to have its effects in our dealings with our environment, the non–ego, just as our relationships with what is outside and beyond self is bound to color our attitude toward self.

> There is constant interplay between the child and the setting in which he finds himself. Both make demands on the other. The child has many fundamental needs which must be satisfied if development is to proceed in a normal, orderly fashion. The environment has many requirements which the child must meet in order that the environment, in turn, will be in a position to satisfy the child's needs. This sounds like argument in a circle, and perhaps it is. At least the argument assumes that there is a constant interplay and interaction of child and environment, and it is the nature of this interaction of forces which interests us at the moment.[52]

[52] J. D. M. Griffin, M.D., *Mental Hygiene: A Manual for Teachers* (New York: American Book Company, 1940), p. 16.

With this important point made to prevent misunderstanding, we will continue our separate treatment of these two aspects of human development to bring them together at a later moment.

Psychologists, perhaps quite rightly inasmuch as they consider themselves scientists rather than philosophers, do not as a rule discuss the nature of man in terms of his fundamental "sociability." The divergence of opinion among the philosophers as to whether man is by nature sociable (following the *Zöon politikon* of Aristotle) or whether he is so by simple contract in a fashion extrinsic to that nature (following Rousseau, Hobbes, Hume, Locke, and the British positivists) is, they say, not their concern.

Nevertheless most of their writings and their attitudes tend to support the first view. For all practical purposes the psychologist considers the relationship of man to his fellow man as a necessary and fundamental part of his nature. As Allers puts it:

> All restriction, crippling, and check to the development of this primal tendency limits man, as we shall show, in the expression of the most representative traits of his character; it renders his participation in the conditions governing natural and supernatural life difficult or even impossible, to a large extent robbing him of his ability to discharge his tasks in either respect. "It is not good for man to be alone"; the creation of woman was coincidently the foundation of the community, the first and original form of which was the family.
>
> As the moral goal of the will to power, when rightly directed, is self–preservation, the development of the sense of personal value, and the complete realization of himself by the individual, so the moral goal of the will to community is love, love of one's neighbor and every other kind of love; for, without presupposing this love, sacrifice and openheartedness cannot exist. The close

> reciprocal interconnection and interaction of these two
> primal or fundamental tendencies of human nature are
> obvious. Neither can develop properly independently
> of the other. If a man were wholly absorbed into the
> community he would lose himself, his individual value
> and his identity; finally, he would no longer be able
> to expend himself for the community, because in fact
> he would cease to exist. In thus losing his value as an
> individual, he would become incapable of loving his
> neighbor; for "thou shalt love thy neighbor as thyself."
> On the other hand, equally, a movement of the will to
> power in the direction of moral and cultural goals is
> rendered impossible—likewise any possible achieve-
> ment—unless a person's will to community is given
> full scope.[53]

This basic need of community means that man cannot develop to
the full without the contact of his fellow men—and the community
in general. This is self–evident in regard to physical, intellectual,
and spiritual things. In the realm of the physical, man could not
live through the first years of his life without the help of others, a
help that is all the more necessary because he follows the law of
nature that postulates slower growth and maturation in proportion
to the higher level of the animal.

In the intellectual realm the achievements of man would be small
indeed were he dependent upon his own resources exclusively and
were he not the heir to the deposit of wisdom and experience of
centuries of his fellow men.

But it is in the psychological sphere that man's dependence upon
man, while more hidden, is most profound and far reaching. This
department of psychology has received its greatest impetus from the

---

[53]   Rudolf Allers, *The Psychology of Character* (New York: Sheed and Ward,
       1935), p. 122. Reprinted with permission of Sheed and Ward.

work of Alfred Adler and his followers who are generally known as the individual psychologists. They have established the basic role of society for the well–being of the individual.

In fact, on the basis of pure psychological research we are able to establish this tendency of human nature as the second basic tendency, second only to the tendency of the ego and its ramifications of self–assertion and development.

To be fully man, the individual must have community. Only in this manner can he develop to his full status. His relationship to community is a necessary and important part of himself. The psychological effects of his relationships to community upon himself are far reaching.

Some psychologists maintain that what most characterizes a child when he is sufficiently advanced to be aware of himself is insecurity. His physical weakness, the uncertainty of his knowledge,[54] the limitations of his abilities, all lead him to fear and worry. In another but very similar manner the adolescent goes through a period of insecurity when he is leaving his childish view of the world to begin to look at it with adult eyes. In both these cases there is only one sure antidote and that is the feeling of belonging to a community, of having a share in a communal effort, of being a part of something greater than self.

In the case of the child, psychologists insist over and over again upon the importance of the community giving the child that sense of belonging.[55] Child psychology insists in season and out of season

[54] See Alters, *op. cit.,* p. 82 — The child who on December 22 was afraid it *might suddenly* be Christmas Eve before his father could return.
[55] Praise and encouragement that are the offshoots of love have effects even on physical energy. Dr. Henry H. Goddard has used a machine to measure fatigue to show that, when an assistant would say "You're doing fine, John" the tired child's energy would soar. The same machine measures the opposite results of fault–finding and discouragement.

on making the child feel secure through love. Love given and love received. He is so small, so ineffective that he cannot contribute anything else. By loving the child, we drive away his fears of not being wanted; by accepting his love we demonstrate to him that he has something to give; he is not a parasite but a very important part of the scheme of things.

In fact, so much stress is laid upon the manifestation of love in childhood that, as in the matters of self–assertion, psychologists often exaggerate. Some would eschew all disapproval under the guise of avoiding discouragement.

Where outside the Christian system can we find the perfect fulfillment of these psychological needs? The basic fact of man's need for companionship is set out in the first words of Holy Scripture. "And the Lord God said: 'It is not good for man to be alone.'"[56] Even in the state of innocence, the fundamental tendency of man to community existed and would have been fulfilled in God's plan without strain or tension between self and nonself.

This fact, known as the solidarity of mankind, has manifested itself in various forms all through the ages. Man has always subconsciously understood his brotherhood with his fellow man, and religious or philosophical theories with some form of human brotherhood as their basis have always had a universal appeal.[57]

---

[56] Gen. 2:18.

[57] This is one of the reasons why Communism presents such a deadly danger. The only basic difference between Communism and the other forms of totalitarianism is in this: Communism does not stress blood ties or nationalism. It is essentially universal and emphasizes the ties of human brotherhood. The class warfare it preaches is not to segregate but to reduce everything to a level in which it can dominate completely.

It is the atheistic and materialistic answer to the Christian concept of brotherhood in the Mystical Body. Because it is systematized and answers a fundamental human drive it is to be reckoned with.

But it required divine inspiration to formulate that solidarity in its highest degree and its boldest vision.[58] Our Lord Himself began that process when He spoke of the vine and the branches. It is true that He is speaking primarily of the relationship of His followers to Himself, but such a relationship postulates the closest intimacy between followers themselves who partake of this common nature and the life of the vine.

It was through St. Paul, however, that the Holy Spirit gave us the full truth, in imagery so vivid that no human theorist had dared even to approach his teachings of human solidarity. Here too the question is raised on the sharing of the life of Christ, but it rapidly turns to the consequences of this union. We are more than blood brothers, we are parts of the same whole, we are members one of the other with the same life flowing through us all.

> For as the body is one
> and hath many members;
> and all the members of the body,
> whereas they are many,
> yet are one body, so also is Christ.

> For as the body is one, and hath many members; and all the members of the body, whereas they are many, yet are one body, so also is Christ.

> For in one Spirit were we all baptized into one body, whether Jews or Gentiles, whether bond or free; and in one Spirit we have all been made to drink.

> For the body also is not one member, but many.

> If the foot should say, because I am not the hand, I am not of the body; is it therefore not of the body?

[58] Even in the Old Testament human brotherhood is taught, but it is obscured through the need of preservation and segregation of the Jewish people.

And if the ear should say, because I am not the eye, I am not of the body; is it therefore not of the body?

If the whole body were the eye, where would be the hearing? If the whole were hearing, where would be the smelling?

But now God hath set the members every one of them in the body as it hath pleased him.

And if they all were one member, where would be the body?

But now there are many members indeed, yet one body.

And the eye cannot say to the hand: I need not thy help; nor again the head to the feet: I have no need of you.

Yea, much more those that seem to be the more feeble members of the body, are more necessary.

And such as we think to be the less honourable members of the body, about these we put more abundant honour; and those that are our uncomely parts, have more abundant comeliness.

But our comely parts have no need: but God hath tempered the body together, giving to that which wanted the more abundant honour,

That there might be no schism in the body; but the members might be mutually careful one for another.

And if one member suffer any thing, all the members suffer with it; or if one member glory, all the members rejoice with it.

Now you are the body of Christ, and members of member.

Careful to keep the unity of the Spirit in the bond of peace.

One body and one Spirit; as you are called in one hope of your calling.

One Lord, one faith, one baptism.

One God and Father of all, who is above all, and through all, and in us all.[59]

Where there is neither Gentile nor Jew, circumcision nor uncircumcision, Barbarian nor Scythian, bond nor free. But Christ is all, and in all. [60]

The psychological implications of such a truth, that we will not develop any further in its doctrinal aspect, are simply tremendous. No human relationship remains unaffected by it.

First, we have the problem of "belonging." It would have been a daring psychologist indeed who would have proposed a unity, a belonging, a participation so close and intimate and all–pervading.

The Christian has here in his hands one of the most consoling doctrines we have ever been given. I do not belong to humanity as a man belongs to a club or even as an individual belongs to a family. I belong to humanity as my hand belongs to me. I am an integral, operative member. The highest form of the life of man, the all–important life of man, sanctifying grace, flows in the Christian, and through it he is in the most intimate contact with all his fellows.

And in teaching this truth it is important to understand, among other aspects, that sanctifying grace is not a life that is superimposed, a sort of extra self or a new faculty. The simplest form of life is the

[59] Eph. 4:3–6.
[60] Col. 3:11. See also: Eph. 5:25–26; Col. 1:9–10; 2:18–19; 1 Cor. 6:15–20; 12:26; Gal. 3:27.

vegetative. The animal does not possess this life plus a new life called sensitive; his sensitive life includes the vegetative. In turn rationality is not added to the sensitive life to make man but the human soul is the principle of life in its vegetative, sensitive, and rational forms depending intrinsically on the body for the first two as a principle of operation, and only extrinsically for the third. In turn sanctifying grace is not just an addition to reason; it is a higher form of life by which we share in the very life of God Himself, and through that participation we are supernaturalized in every part of our being and our action. This is important to realize in the doctrine of the Mystical Body, because we are too inclined to think that this sharing in the life of Christ through the Mystical Body is only a sort of super life that we reach in a vague kind of way in praying or in good deeds, only to fall back to our "normal" manner of being in the ordinary things of life.

Such an error or misconception would spoil most of the psychological value of the doctrine. It would be almost useless to lead a person to feel that he belonged to humanity only in a heavenly sort of way, while perhaps feeling very much out of it in human things. The full meaning of this doctrine must be driven home. Namely, that each individual is meant to form a part of the human unit at the head of which is Christ connecting us with God Himself and joining us one to the other in a union to which every member *must* be important, *must* count for a great deal, *must* have a part to play, because he is a member of a body and like every part of the human body necessary to the proper functioning of the whole.

And this participation has its scope in every situation and at every moment. The fact that the natural is raised to the supernatural does not mean that the "ordinary" things of life are of no importance. On the contrary, it means that everything is of importance in a broader way. The contribution of the individual may seem small and ineffective when judged by purely human standards, but as long as he does his best he is a real dynamic member of the team and he is living a full and useful life whose value will one day be seen by all in God's good time — or eternity.

CHAPTER 7

CHARITY AND ITS
PSYCHOLOGICAL IMPLICATIONS

● ● ●

The problem of love, that is a companion to the problem of belonging, finds its solution also in the Mystical Body. We have said that it is indispensable to every child[61] that he must be loved and that his love be accepted. Brotherly love is such a fundamental principle in Christian teaching that it would seem adequate simply to mention it in order to have its main notions immediately present to the mind.

First among these is that Christian charity is a love based upon unselfishness. Christianity is not required for the other types of love. "Do not the gentiles do this?" (Matt. 5:46). The real test of love, given by Christ Himself, is laying down one's life for one's friend, because then there cannot possibly be any question of selfish motive of a future return from the favored one. The realization of the existence of such a love in the mind of one seeking security and affection in the world, seeking above all to be loved for himself, will establish his confidence in the sincerity of the love of those about him.

---

[61] To every adult also. Man is lost without love. In a great saint the realization of God's love is sufficient to compensate for the loss of all human love, but for most of us to be entirely cut off would be disastrous.

And first and foremost in that community is the loving personality of Christ Himself, the great Lover, who died for His friends, but who by divine power remains still with them to love and comfort them. No natural reasoning or rationalizing can assess the value of the knowledge of the loving Master in the life of any individual. It is a matter of grace and the hidden operation of God in a soul, but anyone who has experienced that saving influence in his own life can realize how the firm basis of confidence, of feeling wanted and loved, can come first and most of all from the loving presence of Christ in our hearts.

From this we can readily appreciate the tremendous psychological importance of presenting God as love, particularly through Christ. What strange aberration, savoring of Jansenism, has led some teachers and some authors to establish the relationship of fear as the predominant one between man and God? We have seen that a false fear is the great danger of childhood. It is also the danger of all other ages. Fear and insecurity can lead to maladjustment and to the devious paths of dangerous forms of compensation. Why then not stress that love that drives out dangerous fear, although reconcilable with the fear that is the beginning of wisdom?

Christ, then, should be first presented as Love. Yet in many widely used catechisms, in answer to many of the questions relating to the fundamental relationships between God and man, there is little or no mention of love as the basic factor.

Another example of the psychological ineptness of our doctrinal approach is the representation of God as an eye! Some may remember such illustrations in their schoolrooms of yester–year. God was introduced not as He who from all eternity had thought of us lovingly, became man out of love, and died on the Cross in the excess of His love; He is not presented as the one who lovingly had formed us, brought us to the life of earth, and the life of grace, surrounded us with His angels and His loving providence. No, not that, not a picture of the Sacred Heart of Love, but a single, grotesque eye. God as a remorseless, implacable, all–seeing eye, awaiting only to find an opportunity to judge and punish the slightest misdemeanor. Perhaps this is good for discipline (although we doubt it), but not for the soul that needs reassurance and the possession of this saving sense of being loved, above all by God who can do all things.

On the purely human side of Christian charity, if we may so speak, because all Christian charity is basically divine, nowhere else is love so complete and so secure. When we are led to under-stand the deep meaning of Christian love, its unselfishness, its history of sacrifice, and heroism in the service of others, there can remain no doubt in the mind struggling for security that we are loved for ourselves and for our own intrinsic God–given worth. There is no sham, no hypocrisy, no self–seeking. The greatest disillusionment that can come to a human being occurs when circumstances lead him to believe that there is nothing true in love and that all men are seekers of their own to the exclusion of all else. Schopenhauer's plea in favor of suicide cannot bring forth any arguments stronger than that.[62] If all devotion, affection, selflessness are so many words, then human nature is a perversion, and nobility of soul, a farce.

But such doubts, such fears are impossible to him who real-izes that all through the ages men and women have followed in the footsteps of the selfless Christ and that today, in spite of all the evil of the world, Christian love still flourishes in the hearts

---

[62] German philosopher Arthur Schopenhauer (1788–1860) held that suicide should not be considered immoral but rather as an assertion of the will to relieve suffering. Schopenhauer further held that suicide could be a rational and even ethical act of the will in people who wish to assert control over the phenomenal world.

of men. The concept of the Mystical Body here again comes into play. Not only are we loved unselfishly by those about us who love us in Christ, but we are in communion with all those all over the world and even in Heaven and in Purgatory in whom pulses the life of Christ.

The poet who wrote the following was a Christian even more than a poet.

The Unknown God

One of the crowd went up,
And knelt before the Paten and the Cup,Received
the Lord, returned in peace and prayed
Close to my side. Then in my heart I said:

"O Christ in this man's life,
This stranger who is Thine in all his strife,
All his felicity, his good and ill,
In the assaulted stronghold of his will,

"I do confess Thee here,
Alive within this life; I know Thee near
Within this lonely conscience, closed away
Within this brother's solitary day.

"Christ in his unknown heart,
His intellect unknown — this love, this art,
This battle and this peace, this destiny
That I shall never know, look upon me!

"Christ in his numbered breath,
Christ in his beating heart and in his death
Christ in his mystery! From that secret place
And from that separate dwelling, give me grace!"[63]

---

[63] Alice Meynell, *The Poems of Alice Meynell* (Toronto: McClelland Stewart, 1923).

Love Accepted

In the relationship to God, rightly conceived, we have also the satisfaction of the psychological need of having our love accepted. (In the child this is particularly important because it is his sole contribution to the community. If he cannot give this he is poor indeed.) Our Lord recognized that need and the human nature behind it when He said, "It is a more blessed thing to give, rather than to receive ."[64] In fact human nature plays some strange tricks in this matter. It is usually by doing things for others that we foster our love for them, and it might be axiomatic to say: "If you wish to make a friend out of an enemy arrange things so that he will do something for you." A popular comic–strip character found himself held to ridiculous obligations to a stranger, because he had saved the stranger's life, and he considered such a tie quite "natcheral."

Impossible though it may sound to non–Christian ears, God, in the depth of His wisdom and His love, has contrived to arrange things in such a manner that He is, in a sense, dependent upon our love. In explaining this, great care must be taken to avoid theological inexactness. It serves no purpose to distort the truth. God is immutable and eternally self–sufficient. The life of the Three in One is in itself beyond the reach of the creature. It does remain true, however, that God has called us to share in His Divine Life and that the key to that participation is our love freely given. God could have made man in such a way that he would have loved him necessarily,[65] and,

---

[64] Acts 20:35.

[65] The theological basis of this truth is that the love of God differs from human love inasmuch as the former creates good where it is bestowed whereas the latter presupposes it. As a consequence, the very love we give God is one of His own gifts and so He crowns His own works. This is the full meaning of the Thomistic thesis that God created man for Himself.

in fact, in our final beatitude we will have no choice but to love the Supreme Good presented to us in the compelling light of the Beatific Vision. But the teaching of the Church and particularly the revelation of the closest friends of God have shown that God is not indifferent to our love, but that He deigns not only to accept it but to desire it. In the Incarnation, of course, this truth becomes more concrete and less hidden. The Sacred Humanity of Christ desires our love as a friend, and the whole story of His life and Passion and death as well as that of His Church is one long appeal for love. Here then we can find an outlet for our love where it is eternally important.

It is also important that man love his fellow men in the same way. No matter what his other limitations, there need be no limitations on his love. St. Thérèse of Lisieux is the patroness of the missions on the same footing as St. Francis Xavier even though she never saw the shores of mission lands.

In the Mystical Body love rules supreme. The love even of a little child can bring souls to Heaven, can convert pagans, can bring down the mercy of God into innumerable hearts. Who then would dare to say that his love of his fellow men in God is unimportant?

If this concept can be driven home, the greatest possible contribution has been made to proper adjustment to community. No longer is it possible to wonder if we belong. We are full–fledged members upon whom God Himself depends to complete the work of His redemption.

CHAPTER 8
CHARITY AND BEING GODLIKE

• • •

The song writer has said, "For 'tis love and love alone the world is seeking,"[66] and he said it well. Under many guises, through many vicissitudes and innumerable bypaths, the human heart seeks for love.

It is an urge so universal, so profound, so all–absorbing that we must trace its origin to the Creator of man. Again we must recall those words so full of significance and consequence, "Let us make man to our image and likeness."[67]

From all eternity God contemplates Himself and in that timeless intellectual act generates His Idea of Himself, the Word, the Son, the Second Person of the Trinity.

And the Father and the Son in their mutual knowledge are locked in the mutual embrace whence proceeds the Spirit, the personalized Love of God.

In creating man to His own image and likeness God makes man a being with powers of intellectual knowledge and spiritual love. In raising man to the supernatural order God places those powers on a new level, gives them a new direction, a new objective, a new

---

[66] Herbert, Victor and Johnson Young, Rida. *Ah, Sweet Mystery of Life.* 1910.
[67] Gen. 1:26.

participation, namely, the ability now to share in the very knowledge and love that God has of Himself in the eternal processes of the Trinity.

The love, then, that man is seeking is primarily the love of God, "Thou shalt love the Lord thy God . . ."[68] This truth is so sublime we tend to underplay it. To give only one example, we speak often of the results of grave sin as though God withdraws His love from the sinner as a form of punishment. This is only partially true. The essence of mortal sin is that we choose something other than God, forbidden to us here and now, and prefer it to God. This is an act of love. We place a higher value on a creature than we do on God. We love that creature more. But God by nature must love Himself supremely, above all else. As a result, when we raise a creature above God in our scale of values, we have ceased to be Godlike. We ourselves have resisted the current of true love. It is not necessary for God to "withdraw." We ourselves have destroyed our true supernatural charity or love since we no longer love Him as He loves Himself, namely, in a supreme fashion that can brook no rival.

The secret, then, of our truest, deepest, only perfect love is in being Godlike. And as the second great commandment is like unto the first, it is also the standard, the norm, and the criterion of our love for our fellow men.

It would be impossible to follow out this thought in all its applications and implications. We have taken one such problem, partly because it is so psychological in nature, partly because it is one of the most difficult and most mysterious areas in which we must seek the outward expression of this "being Godlike." If we can achieve it here, it should be possible in all else.

---

[68] Matt. 22:37.

Pain and Punishment

The mystery of pain in the world has always puzzled even the most submissive of God's children and the most illuminated by grace. It seems like a contradiction to say that God is omnipotent and that He loves us and at the same time admit that He has created a world in which we suffer so cruelly.

And when it comes to the question of being obliged, ourselves, to inflict suffering on others under guise of punishment, we sometimes wonder even more and tend to rebel. It may then be rewarding to study some of the principles that should guide the Christian in his attitude to punishment, particularly where children are involved.

Once the child enters into his kingdom, once he understands and accepts his true position in the community, the way is paved for overcoming many of the difficulties that usually are such a problem between the youth and the adult.

Let us take as an example the problem of punishment, that is a major one in youth education. We have said that there is exaggeration in the writings of some psychologists because under the guise of avoiding inhibitions in the young they adopt a *laissez–faire* attitude that practically excludes the use of punishment. The Christian abhors the concept of pain for pain's sake, but a look at the world tells him that the surest guarantee of future pain may be its avoidance here and now. The "spoiled" child, overshielded against pain, may be the one who will ultimately suffer the most. The child must be taught that misbehavior, even carelessness, will bring with it pain and suffering. It is the lesson of life, and to have a child pass through the formative period without learning that lesson thoroughly would be a grievous harm. It is the only concrete realization he can get of the terrible effects of sin. On the other hand, punishment mismanaged can do tremendous psychological harm. It tends to increase the distance between the adult and the child, a distance that already terrifies him and increases his insecurity. Applied with a lack of consistency[69] it upsets his nascent ideas of order and justice and leads him to seek devious ways to avoid retribution that seems based rather on the humor of the adult than on any objective moral code.

But punishment that is part of a truly Christian education not only is not harmful but positively beneficial. The condition is, however, that it be truly in accordance with Christian principles. This involves the general background of love that we have just described. It also involves the proper use of punishment itself. That proper use we would sum up as follows: To be as Godlike as possible in administering punishment.

When God punishes there are always several factors involved. The first and perhaps most fundamental of these is that the punishment is always objective, that is, based entirely upon the guilt of the offender.

This is in direct opposition to the human legal position that obtains in our courts of law to the effect that "ignorance of the law is no excuse," and that is necessary lest every criminal escape by a plea of ignorance. Man cannot always "scrutinize the heart." A good judge tries to take the objective elements into consideration within the limitations of the statutes, but he will be the first to admit that human justice is not always accurate.

But God proceeds differently. His judgment is entirely based upon the personal guilt of the culprit. His punishment is consistent and with knowledge could be foretold. Sentiment, passion, favoritism, none of these factors enter in. And from Him we must learn

---

[69] Examples:
  a) The parent who punishes the child for acting in a certain way before visitors when the same conduct had hitherto been tolerated or even encouraged.
  b) The teacher who punishes for hitherto accepted forms of conduct because *he* was out late the night before.

our lesson. Children do not so much fear punishment as they are upset by injustice or at a loss through inconsistency. From adults whom they trust and in whose love they have complete confidence punishment is not a fearful thing. They themselves know that they are guilty and to what extent. When they know that their parent or teacher is trying to the best of his human ability to assess that guilt and to punish in consequence, they accept quite easily and without psychological disturbance the results of their misdemeanor. But if the adult is not Godlike in his punishment; if his yardstick is the state of his temper, the damage done (perhaps accidentally) to his pet possessions, the person of the culprit, his offended dignity, or some other petty and perhaps sinful consideration, then the child's resentment, anger, and perhaps his hatred is aroused. St. Paul has a most pertinent text that Pope Pius XI quoted in his encyclical on *Christian Education:* "Fathers, do not provoke your children to anger."[70] People who do not think too much on the subject are surprised at the form of that precept. They think that it should be the other way around. But the Apostle knew that greater harm would come by provoking the child to anger because in the child's soul such wounds are deep and lasting.

Another Godlike characteristic of punishment is His accent in this world on the medicinal aspects of His penalties.

There are three main reasons for punishment. First of all, it seeks to restore a damaged order and hence is called retributive.[71] In the

---

[70] Eph. 6:4.

[71] Retributive punishment is sometimes called "vindictive." It is in this sense that Scripture puts into the mouth of God the words "Revenge is mine — I shall repay." But this is better called retributive because it stresses God's intention to right all wrong, to restore all order. True vindictive punishment, that is the search for personal satisfaction for a wrong, has no place in the life of the Christian. Witness the Church's ban on dueling.

realm of physics there is a principle that "to every force there is a contrary and equal force." So it is in the moral order. Retribution must follow sooner or later.

Punishment, in human affairs, may also be protective in scope. It is with this in mind that we sometimes isolate human beings from their fellows because their continued freedom would constitute a threat to the security of the individual and the State.

Finally, punishment is medicinal. The term itself is sufficiently expressive. It stems from eternal optimism in the face of human frailty. No one need be despaired of; all are within the framework of mercy.

In human affairs all these aspects must be present. First, the retributive. The child must be led to realize the effect of his actions upon the moral order. Physical damage is relatively unimportant. Worldly people judge by physical damage, and the rule is that if sin is hidden it is not sin. Children must learn that their every action has its effect. The effect in the moral world is like that produced by a stimulus in the neural pathways of the body that jealously preserve its every effect. As James has so well said:

> We are spinning our own fates, good or evil, and never to be undone. Every smallest stroke of virtue or vice leaves its never–so–little scar. The drunken Rip Van Winkle, in Jefferson's play, excuses himself for every fresh dereliction by saying "I won't count this time!" Well, he may not count it, and a kind Heaven may not count it, but it is being counted none the less. Down among his nerve cells and fibres the molecules are counting it, registering and storing it up to be used against him when the next temptation comes. Nothing we ever do is, in strict scientific literalness, wiped out.[72]

[72] William James, *The Philosophy of William James* (New York: Random House, n. d.), p. 285.

Punishment in the Christian sense should be presented as a restorative of the moral order that has been damaged. It is something to be accepted willingly, even gladly, in order that the damage may be undone. For this reason it is good to keep the punishment in the line of guilt because there again it is Godlike to make the punishment fit the crime.

The protective element of punishment, while less striking, requires understanding. God uses it, although often in mysterious ways. If we could see the divine plan we might have better insight into some of the events that we label as tragedies. A premature death, the incapacitation of a seemingly indispensable person, an enforced separation—how many of these tragedies are perhaps blessings—a punishment, perhaps—but also surely in many cases a protection. The lovers Dona Prouheze and Don Rodriguez in Claudel's *Satin Slipper* find it impossible ever to meet because the former, a married woman, has put her shoe in the hands of the Virgin and prayed that when she would try to rush to evil that it would be "with a limping foot." And so they are punished and protected all at once.

But it is the third aspect, the medicinal, that must be stressed. Christian punishment, outside of eternal damnation, is actually a gesture of confidence. That is a startling truth and one we are seldom brought to realize. God consistently and continuously punishes us for our own good. The Old Testament is a record of the continuous succession of punishments by which the Almighty kept His chosen people in the line of conduct set for them. Our own lives bear witness to the salutary lessons of Divine Mercy that lie hidden under the unattractive wrapping of pain and suffering.

What a different color punishment takes on when we realize that it is really a part of love. When it is brought home that "he does not bother who does not care," that it is because of an unbounded confidence in our ability to do better that we are feeling a corrective that may sting but that will also heal. But to that end we must really have love and patience. And we must not be afraid to explain. Children will feel this instinctively in an adult who is really motivated by love for them, but that is not enough. It is essential that their realization be made positive and conscious. Then will they feel all the more loved, all the more a part of the community, and punishment instead of being a terror and a psychological disturbance will be a support and an aid to Christian living and Christian understanding of life and the love of God, and of man, His image. "Whom the Lord loveth, He chastizeth."[73]

[73] Heb. 12:6.

CHAPTER 9

CHARITY AND LEARNING TO GIVE

● ● ●

We have already mentioned the need of the doctrine of Original Sin to understand the psychological make–up of the individual. In community relationships Original Sin also comes into play. The full reason why community and contact with our fellow men can help us become reconciled with our lot is that we are of Adam's stock, a race of wounded beings who have tendencies to evil. We are not intrinsically evil, as some of the Reformers would have it, but we have precarious control of ourselves and have a penchant for getting into trouble. This means that the failure of the individual, his struggles, and his temptations are not his alone, but the lot of every man.

The tendency of self–assertion, that the individual psychologists so well term the "will to power," would rapidly run riot if it were not for community relationships. It is very interesting to observe the developing spirit of cooperation, the "social spirit" in the growth of a child. With very young children, socialized play is practically nonexistent; the drive to power has not yet been coordinated and fitted into the community scheme. What actually happens in attempts at socialized play is that the strongest or the most dominant has his way and plays as he chooses. The others follow or the game disintegrates. It is very often the latter. There is practically no team play. The boy who owns the bat and ball will usually insist on being the pitcher, and if he is not humored he takes his possessions and goes home. It is very difficult to lead anyone to play in a subordinate position. Any adult who has had experience organizing play among young children will appreciate these facts.

Here, then, we have the will to power relatively unchecked; were it to continue so the individual would be a misfit or society itself would disintegrate.

But fortunately social pressure exercises its own force to counteract and control the assertive tendencies of the individual. For example, there is considerable pleasure in socialized play. Competitive games are challenging and stimulating and the contact with others attractive. The child soon learns of these pleasures and comes to realize that if he is to enjoy them he must accept the rules and cooperate; if necessary, he must accept a subordinate position in order that the game may go on.

And so it is in the game of life. The will to power in the well–adjusted adult accepts the limitations imposed upon it, and the individual curbs his assertiveness so that he may be a proper member of society, whether it take the form of family, industry, country, or the broadest community of humanity itself. And only when he is properly adjusted to all these manifestations of community and all the others of his life is he really a perfect man, a perfect adult. Otherwise he remains in varying degrees a child. We have all met these childish adults who are unable to adjust themselves to the demands of society, who, as soon as a situation imposes unwanted restriction upon them, react violently and passionately, like a child in a tantrum, or withdraw into their shell and refrain from further participation like a child taking his ball and bat and going home.

But these are examples of maladjustment. When the community with its restricting influence has been accepted, the individual finds therein a most beneficial curb to excess in his will to power.

Anyone who has been trained in the Christian school of charity and willingness to sacrifice will readily recognize how completely the standard it fosters measures up to the requirements of sound psychological adjustment in this matter. The will to power, that has so strong a tendency to get out of hand, is under continuous curb in the Christian scheme of self–sacrificing charity.

The child, who by nature begins by being unsocial (in the sense defined above), if properly trained in Christian behavior, is led from his earliest days to renounce himself in favor of others. In the first contacts with community, that usually resolves itself to his parents and his brothers and sisters, he is taught that God expects him to put himself after others. Humility and faith teach him his proper place, and he realizes that all his greatness is due to God's gift. He recognizes as well that these divine gifts require him to think first of others. The true concept of charity leaves him no doubt of his being loved and of the importance of his love to others, but there must be no species of weakness in this and so he is led to accept the curbs imposed upon him by his membership in the community. This work, of course, cannot be done in a day. For that matter, it is the work of a lifetime, but it is surprising the amount of cooperation that can be established even among young children when the proper Christian motivation is used. In fact, just as we have adults who are children psychologically, a great deal of psychological maturity and adjustment can be obtained through Christian attitudes even in the young.

THE PSYCHOLOGICAL IMPORT OF CHRISTIAN IDEALISM

CHAPTER 10

IDEALS AND HUMAN BEHAVIOR

● ● ●

It is reported that when the Scots were fighting the Saracens in Spain, they had brought with them the heart of their beloved Robert Bruce and their battle technique consisted in throwing his heart before them and then battling onward until they recovered it.

The story may or may not be true, but the symbolism is very apt. Many personalities do not develop as much as they should because they lack objectives or because they have not continued to set up higher and higher objectives as life progresses.

Educational psychology is filled with chapters on motivation, incentives, ideals, ambition, and kindred subjects. Depth psychologists and psychiatrists tell us that the will to live and to accomplish is absolutely necessary for mental health and that one of the hardest types of pathological cases is that of the man or woman who has lost the desire to go forward and consequently to live.

But the greatest difficulty in dealing with this topic is precisely that these two groups (the educational psychologist and the clinical or depth psychologist) are, generally speaking, on two different levels. The depth psychologist is usually concerned with the unconscious and its effect upon attitude and action. On this level it is, in practice, useless to discuss the formation of ideals as such because if therapy is required it must be applied by the expert who can reach into the unconscious and bring up the motivation that must be recognized and rationalized before any other step is contemplated.

The description of such therapy or the role of ideals or motivation therein is not within the scope of this discussion. We are convinced that what we propose can by indirection be valuable in all cases, but it must be made clear that we speak primarily of the conscious level.

Applied psychology has established, then, the need for what we will call ideals without, for the moment, any further definition. But it is the duty of the Christian psychologist and educator to scan the rational basis for such findings. Moreover, this matter plays such an important role in the formation of youth that it is vital to have clear ideas on the fundamental problem involved and above all to clear away several faulty notions that are prevalent in educational circles.

In order to do this, let us glance briefly at what is involved in the basic psychology of motivation and consequently of idealism.

Motivation is the presentation of reasons for attitude or action. It is, then, primarily a stimulus to the action of the will. Thus, the basic educational question of will power comes to the forefront. What is this thing called will power? A vast number of people, among them many educators, seem to think that will power is a sort of permanent ability to use the will in a certain highly developed fashion. The general impression seems to be that will power grows like muscular power and that once a person becomes "strong–willed" it is sufficient to present the proper occasion to elicit the correct response. And as the will is a spiritual faculty that power must be universal and extend itself to all forms of action. This matter must not be confused with the acquisition of habits by repeated acts, that obviously implies greater ease of action. We here refer to the idea that the will itself becomes developed and thus gives us a "strong–willed" person in all circumstances. By this development a strong–willed person would always be strong–willed because the will is involved in all deliberate action.

But is it so in life? If the will itself be so developed, can we explain the evident weaknesses in persons who have always exercised a great deal of strong willing in difficult circumstances, and the amazing power of people who have seldom "willed" (in this sense) because they have always given in to themselves, who at a certain moment may exercise outstanding fortitude even though it may be on a purely natural scale. Let us take some examples. In the first category we have the virtuous people who may even have given up all things and who lead a life of daily mortification and self–sacrifice. If ever will power as such could be developed they would have it. Yet in practically all of these lives, as anyone experienced in the ascetical life will readily testify, there is some weak point or weak points. It may be the rule of silence, it may be morning rising, or some point of obedience, but almost inevitably the weakness is there and effort after effort, retreat after retreat are brought to bear upon the deficiencies. Again, immediately after a retreat virtue is at a very high tide. Is it because will power was developed during those few days? Hardly that, because given the continued effort of the first days after retreat, that will power would go forward and we would inevitably go from victory to victory until the next retreat. Universal experience must sadly reject so glowing a proposition.

On the other hand there are the delinquents, the sinners, those who have sought pleasure all their lives and for whom it is usually sufficient for a thing to be difficult to be avoided. Therefore, by definition, they should not have developed will power. Yet suddenly they may go through fire and water even for some trifling advantage. Lindworsky gives these examples:

In Munich, it was not unusual to see fifteen– to seventeen–year–old girls standing at daybreak in wind and rain, in line before the Royal Theatre. These girls certainly may be credited with very considerable achievements in waiting there from five, four or even three o'clock in the morning, and, occasionally even from the previous evening, until the box office opened at nine in the morning. All they were after was an inexpensive ticket. And, yet, they were not heroes of will power.

I remember a former pupil who was regarded by his teachers as a person of typically weak will — a really weak man. The boy had, however, an ideal, that of becoming a smart army officer. Many a person who observed this weakly young man seriously doubted the sincerity of his ideal. And still, in spite of a very great obstacle which would have caused others to change their choice of profession, he reached his objective. During the war he performed heroic deeds, which cannot be described here without identifying a living man. It would not be difficult to cite many historic cases of this kind which justify us in drawing the following conclusion: Everybody who is capable of conceiving a high aim can become a hero and can achieve deeds which are expected only of a strong will, even if he has not the general quality of will power.[74]

And in our own surroundings, what of the men and women who will stand all day and all night to see a sporting event or a parade. Are they the strong–willed in a general sense? It is to be doubted.

The only thing remaining is to clarify our ideas of the source of will power. St. Thomas has referred to the will as a "blind

[74] Johann Lindworsky, S.J., *Training of the Will* (Milwaukee: Bruce Publishing, 1929), p. 45.

power." The will acts accordingly as it is guided by the intellect.[75] In other words, the intellect furnishes motives for action — here is the source of "motivation." "Nothing is willed unless it is first known." And with that all the pieces fall into place. The religious has his or her little weaknesses because on that score the intellect does not furnish sufficient motivation to induce the correct action of the will. Retreats are effective immediately afterward because the intellect is in full contemplation of the superior motivation it has fostered during those days. And as the world rushes in and other motivation gradually becomes uppermost, action and virtue may suffer. On the other hand, even though effort is not a man's strong point, he may see sufficient reason even for heroic action, and because the motivation is so strong he will follow its lead.

It would be erroneous to deduce from this that good action is useless in itself as a builder of character. For the sake of clarity, let us distinguish three areas of action: the *unmotivated*; the *motivated only*; the *mixed*.

The "*unmotivated*": There are levels of conduct where objective motivation may be dispensed with, yet where habit may be valuable. Let us take orderliness and cleanliness as examples. It is of little use to preach to a little boy on such subjects. The value of being clean is obscure for him. He will be clean only if obliged. But that obligation rapidly becomes a necessity through experience and he awakens one day to find uncleanness repugnant. The same is true of orderliness. Keeping one's "things" in order is seldom an innate characteristic. But, if it is authoritatively imposed as a habit from youth, it too can become a necessity. In school certain drill subjects, "number facts," for example, fall into this category.

---

[75] St. Thomas, *Summa Theologiae*, I–II, q. 50, art. 2.

Therefore, it is true to say that there is an area where pure action or habit is beneficial.

The "*motivated only*": In other matters, action without any intrinsic motivation is almost a waste of time and energy and may even be harmful. In some religious boarding schools the obligatory attendance at certain nonobligatory religious functions (like Vespers) with the motivation of "Never–mind–why, you'll–go–because–you're–told" has left some otherwise normally religious adults with an irrational dislike for that particular form of piety. It is an interesting point to debate whether obligatory attendance at Mass on weekdays falls into this category or the next.

The habit of personal prayer is one that can be achieved only through motivation, and in general the same may be said for the acquisition of most virtues. They cannot be "imposed"; they can be gained only through properly motivated action.

The "*mixed*" area: At other times action that is both imposed and motivated is necessary, particularly in forming habits that will remain as touchstones for external conduct. For example, to allow children to go to Sunday Mass or confession only "if they choose" would be disastrous. Here the habit must be acquired even if imposed, but it *must* be accompanied by intrinsic motivation. The repeated act itself would be next to useless. To become a life value and a life pattern, its imposition must be made palatable by continued and properly adapted motivation and explanation.

From this we can see very clearly the tremendous importance of ideas, of motives, and consequently of ideals in the formation of character, particularly during the formative and plastic periods of childhood and youth. And this realization leads to a modification of our approach to the problem of discipline. Action for the sake of action is useless, because there is really no such thing. But we will take this up again when speaking of supernatural motivation.

For the moment the point is that for successful guidance and for worthwhile living there have to be motives. In other words, there must be "ideals" to be sought.

The absence of such adequate motivation can lead us to two types of maladjustment. First, there is the person who for some reason, let us say the loss of a loved one or a defeat of some kind, considers that there is nothing further to be gained by life or at any rate that there is no purpose in making efforts to set up and seek values that we term worthwhile. In acute cases this can lead to suicide. Suicide is always a psychological disaster and indicates that a negative scale of values has triumphed over a positive one. Freud bases suicide upon a fundamental urge known as the death drive that is opposed to the drive to life and that causes suicide when it becomes predominant. Unconscious motivation is also at work in such action and, when the disadvantages of life are accepted as overweighing the advantages, there is danger that suicide may take place.

But suicide is an extreme case. What usually happens is that, as we have said, the person no longer has any wish to build personality, to develop abilities, but drags out a pitiful existence, seeking material and frequently sensuous pleasures as they are offered without any desire for further goals.

In such advanced cases we may be reasonably sure that we are dealing with persons of at least neurotic condition. Professional psychological help is needed to deal with the unconscious motivation. The presentation of prayer, ideals, and incentives will not likely be effective until the hidden wound has been cleansed and at least partly healed.

There is, however, another type of maladjustment based on the lack of proper ideals or motivation. It is exemplified in a person who fears defeat in seeking further and is content to rest on his laurels. This condition is very general and exists in varying degrees in all of us. Self–examination makes us sufficiently conscious of it at this level to take positive steps to help eradicate it. When we have reached a modicum of success in some field we are usually tempted not to do any more but to take an independent attitude and to satisfy ourselves by thinking and speaking of how much more we could have accomplished had we wished to try. There follows a withdrawing from competition and afterward a bitterness or a deprecatory attitude toward the success of others. How often we hear people sneering at the success of others with remarks such as these: "Well, look how he studies." — or, "Yes, but he is ruining his health." — or, "Who would want it if he had to be like that?" — or, "What price glory?" These are very often indications of a refusal to press forward because proper motivation and idealism are lacking.

What is the remedy proposed by psychology? There are many, and we do not pretend to do them entire justice. But it is our point that as long as they remain on the natural plane they cannot fully succeed, and that Christian idealism offers the same values with additional ones as well.

To be effective, character or personality building must have a *basic level of motivation.* Here we treat of ideals properly so called. For the needs of the moment, temporary or superficial motivation is obviously necessary and quite effective. Thus a threatening adult with a strong arm may be all that is required to make a child engage in virtuous activity at a given point. But this does not fulfill our real requirements. What is needed under this heading is an objective scale of values to which all such secondary and temporary motivation may be adjusted.

This motivation must be in terms of life *values.* To be effective against the "slings and arrows of outrageous fortune," against the emotional low points and dark days, life itself must have a goal. The whole has to be presented as greater than its parts, and the value of living and being as greater than any partial setback in life however great. Psychologists consequently build up the motivation of the personality in some of the terms we have set forth in the first section. The character of irreplaceability of every individual, the great positive values of the proper use and development of the whole personality with all its attendant functions, the joy of the simple things in life, like the beauty of nature and the glow of health, the abiding happiness of human love, of intellectual search, of artistic endeavor, all these things are offered as life values and motivation for continued forward effort, or in other words as ideals.

Finally, this motivation must be *permanent*. A scale of values that stands up only under given conditions cannot serve as a basis upon which to build one's life. A great deal of the unhappiness in the world exists precisely because so few actually have fundamental values to which they can cling when things go wrong. The search for praise or pleasure or power may suffice for a time, but the day will inevitably come when the full glare of life's inexorable light will reveal the tinsel quality of such baubles.

Particularly in dealing with youth must such permanence dominate in the values that are offered. Psychologists are quick to decry the prevalence of purely transient motivation in education. They show that high grades, for example, are an insufficient motive from a personality–building point of view. Since this motive lacks permanence, it is ineffective. In after–school life there will be no grades, and success will have to be interpreted in different terms. They insist, then, that emphasis be laid upon the effort expended, not on the grade achieved, because it is in accordance with the qualitative not the quantitative rendition that true success is to be defined.

There can be no doubt about the soundness of these findings. But we maintain that such motivation, such ideals, as are here sought cannot be found on the natural plane but require the level of Christian idealism.

To sum up, we are told that we must find a basic level of motivation, an objective scale to which all secondary motives may be referred; the ideal must be in terms of life value and, of course, permanent.

What of the Christian ideal? If the psychologist has no spiritual view he usually tears down by his philosophy of life what his positive science has built up. How can there be an objective scale of values unless that scale is anchored on something outside self—yes, even outside mankind and the created universe? The natural law with its acceptance of God as the Author of "things as they are" and consequently the explanation of their *raison d'être* is the only possible basis for an objective scale. Things must be sought because they are the proper object of our search and correspond to the manner in which we are created and are designed to operate.

In the matter of life value, what is there that can really sustain us in all circumstances of life except the concept of God as our Father? For many, there are trials and sorrows so deep and soul–searing that nothing short of the concept of eternity and an infinite healing can help in the day of tribulation. Besides, the very wear of living gets too monotonous. The emptiness of human values above becomes all too apparent once we have passed through the rosy hopes of adolescence and youth. There is not any man who has ever lived who cannot say with Solomon "vanity of vanities, and all is vanity," or as it should be translated, "emptiness of emptiness and all is emptiness."[76] For the psychologist who does not believe in another world it must be a difficult task indeed to try to convince his patient that life is worth living. At times, it must be still harder to convince himself.

[76] Eccles. 1:2.

The permanence of motivation requires the same supernatural theme. And this is of the utmost importance to the Christian. It is not sufficient to have the action performed here and now. The main purpose of training the will through obedience or constructing virtuous habits is not to provide an atmosphere for study, nor yet to train in blind obedience, but rather to perfect in the search for good *because it is good*. But, as we have said, we must *know* it is good if we are to search for it. Therefore, the reasons must be given. And the reasons must belong to good as good. Otherwise from a character viewpoint it is wasted. If the reason is simply to please another, to get a good mark in school, or some other reward, and if these partial motives are not connected with permanent ones, then they will have no effect when they are no longer present, that may be as soon as the next day.

The love of God, both eternal and incarnate, His glory, the obtaining of virtue and merit for Heaven, the acquiring of grace and protection against future temptation, these are all motives that are permanent. They are never displaced or lost through the shifting circumstances of life. In connection with the formation of good religious habits they are the only motives that are of value. In other connections they should always be the basis or, if you prefer, the center to which all other temporary and partial motives are referred.

"A man's reach should exceed his grasp, or what's a heaven for."[77] We all know that our reach does exceed our grasp. We don't have to be psychologists to know the keen hunger for the infinite, the wave of loneliness that breaks over us when we have time to stop and think and sometimes when we haven't. As Plato said, "This every soul seeketh and for the sake of this doth all her actions, having an inkling that it is; but what it is she cannot sufficiently discern,

[77] Browing, Robert. "Andrea del Sarto."

and she knoweth not her way, and concerning this she hath no constant assurance as she hath of other things."[78] We know that we are made for much more than anything that we can possess here, and as long as the best held out to us is some earthly value our hearts are ever restless. On the other hand, peace and hope and an abiding trust take possession of us when we can say, "I know whom I have believed,"[79] and we can even go on with St. Paul and say, "I exceedingly abound with joy in all our tribulation."[80] There are never suicides among the saints.

[78] Plato, *Republic,* VI, 501 d 11–e3.
[79] 2 Tim. 1:12.
[80] 2 Cor. 7:4.

CHAPTER 11

NATURE OF CHRISTIAN IDEALS—THEIR CHOICE AND PRESENTATION

● ● ●

But what of the ideals themselves that should be held forth to him who would lead a full life? The foregoing has permitted us to clarify our ideas on the basic psychological significance of such ideals, their effect upon action and their fundamental prerequisites. We now wish to establish a little more concisely and concretely the nature of such ideals and how they should be chosen and presented.

Lindworsky says: "The ideal is nothing less than a value, a motive; however, with this peculiarity that this value is a complete value, a complex motive in which all the motives required for the particular pupil are contained."[81] In this sense it is a synthesis of motives into one whole, represented by a type of character or even a person real or imaginary. When speaking of presenting ideals to youth we mean setting up objectives for them to attain, giving them the reasons for attaining them, and showing them models or examples of others who have done so. The ideal, then, really is a type of end result that personality–building seeks to produce.

A great deal of care must be exercised to prevent falsifying the Christian ideal itself and consequently the ideals of the Christian.

---

[81] Johann Lindworsky, S.J., *Training of the Will* (Milwaukee: Bruce Publishing, 1929), p. 137.

The author of the *Imitation* states: "It is inevitable that even religious hearts will acquire a coating of worldly dust,"[82] and I have heard a priest challenge his class of Catholic boys and girls whether or not they were pagans. His criterion was: "What do you look forward to in your lives? A prosperous marriage, a home beyond the golf course, success and adulation? Yet, we call ourselves followers of Christ. Did He have these things?" He was only too correct in his assessment. Our ideal of success is not Christian; often enough we pay for it through inflicting psychological wounds on ourselves.

What should we present as the ideal of success to young people? Tangible results? It is the world that demands this type of success. "The world loves a winner." God requires only that we try. But we must do that. Our school system of marks starts us out on the wrong foot. We seem to judge success by achievement, seldom by effort. We put a premium on sheer brain power, on memory, or any other measurable quality. But God does not. The man who doubled the two talents was rewarded exactly as the man who doubled five. Our reward in Heaven will be in accord with our *love,* therefore with the effort of will we have expended, not in accord with the success of our efforts in any concrete way.

The first thing, then, is to insist, in season and out of season, upon the true ideal of success. What peace it can bring to those who have not the gifts of their companions. And what a safeguard to the brilliant leaders who are not permitted to rest on their own oars and be satisfied because they can get by easily. Heaven must be won "and the violent carry it away."[83] Thus will be avoided the double pitfall, that of leading the less gifted to an exaggerated feeling of inferiority with all the dangerous forms of compensation that may go with it, and that of presenting a perfect opportunity

---

[82] *"Necesse est de mundano pulvere etiam religiosa corda sordescere."*
[83] Matt. 11:12.

for the more gifted to retire from the battle of life after a few trifling successes.

In speaking of the choice of ideals and their presentation to the young we must stress the dominant note of the value of the individual. We have already pointed out that the sacredness of the individual is a fundamental point in Christian teaching. Here, too, the same truth must be kept in mind.

Very often in holding up ideals we forget that God did not make anyone like anyone else. It is one of the marvels of His power that He has been able to create so many people and not any two are truly the same. We must realize His plan in diversity.

As a consequence, it is poor theology and bad psychology to hold up any human being as an *absolute* ideal for another. How often we hear parents, using the boy next door or down the street as the yardstick by which all actions are judged and as the ultimate goal of perfection to strive for. "Why can't you be like so–and–so. He wouldn't soil his clothes like that; he never fails in his examinations," or he possesses whatever virtue chances to be under discussion. Teachers sometimes follow a similar line with some variations. Some have been known to hold individuals up as models for all to imitate. Parents sometimes hold up an elder son or daughter as a model.

It is quite obvious that this line of conduct is, first of all, imprudent. Children know much more about the "model child" referred to, above all that he is no model. This makes the parent or teacher sound very ridiculous and unfair. Again it is the surest way to develop hatreds and enmities among people.

But that is only secondary to our discussion. The main thing is that no one is supposed to be patterned after his neighbor. Each has his own faults and his own qualities, temperament, and characteristics. His ideal is the development of all his God–given powers to do the best with what he has.

The danger of psychological damage is much greater here when the ideal continually thrown in one's face is the dominant personality in his environment. This serves only to accentuate a general feeling of inferiority, incompetency, and inability ever to live up to what someone else, say a relative, has set as a standard.

The best illustration of this is in the case of the children of famous parents. It is simply inhuman and certainly un–Christian to keep on telling a child that he or she will never be a success like father. The worst of it is that the child is already convinced of that fact. All through life they have been known not as John Smith or Mary Brown like the other children of their age. They have never been known for themselves at all. They have been not "substances" but "relationships." "This is the son of Senator X or Governor Y or General B." And while they stand there everyone about them gushes, not over them, but over the merits of the famous father. The scene usually ends by the poor child being told not to forget to work hard and grow up just like his dad. The very favors or privileges he or she too often receives from doting teachers or other adults are bitter because they are all a part of the overwhelming load of someone else's fame, that must be carried and under which the child's personality is submerged and lost.

A fourteen–year–old son of a famous father seemed to be of a rather quiet temperament. He had, of course, been well brought up and was superficially very polite. However, when left to himself among the other boys he was extremely arrogant, insisted on being the leader in all activities, swaggered, and boasted of his achievements, past, present, and future. When someone gained his confidence and mentioned his unusual and undesirable behavior to his companions, he finally admitted that he really had no desire to be like that at all. "But," he added, "I have to." The reason for his strange obligation he gave as follows: "Nobody pays any attention to *me*. They only think and talk about my dad. The only thing they tell me is that I have to be like him. But I don't know how to be like him and I have never accomplished anything anyway. So I make things up and boast about them. And I try to be a leader like him by bossing the others around. I wish I had an ordinary father; it would be so much easier,"

The case speaks for itself. The utter futility of trying to make people in the same mold is apparent. All that is achieved is heartache and warped personality. Added to this is something the lad did not see himself but was quite clearly present, i.e., the submerged personality clamors for recognition and will strive for it, if not by fair means, then by foul.

However, it must not be concluded that there is no proper way to hold up an individual as a model to be imitated or an ideal to be sought. This practice, widespread in education, particularly in the fields of religion, literature, and history, is a laudable one and has a sound psychological appeal. That appeal is based upon the tendency to insecurity that is in all of us and is particularly manifest in childhood and adolescence. As we have said, life has its terrors for us and we feel doubtful of our ability to face its dangers and to come safely through them with any measure of success. It is consequently extremely comforting and reassuring to know that our blood brothers, others of this same feeble mortal clay, have walked the same road and have passed not only safely but gloriously through the same perils that beset us now. The classical example is that of St. Augustine and his famous motto: "If these can, why can't I?"

The Church recognizes this human tendency to the fullest in its liturgy. The Church year is richer in saints than it is in days. The whole doctrine of the communion of saints, the custom of patrons for nations, for arts and trades, and for almost every situation in life, saints' names for individuals—all these things bear witness to the Church's endorsement of a tradition that is of considerable educational importance.

But even here, as Allers points out so well, prudence must be exercised in the ideal presented. He writes:

> A young mechanic should not choose Julius Caesar, nor a tax–collector Napoleon, as his ideal figure. St. Catherine of Siena is not a suitable example for girls of our time, and the life of a solitary is not an ideal for the realities of modern social and economic conditions. We may add to this that the lives of most of the saints, as they are described for us, are quite remote from all actuality, not only from ours but also from that of the saint; compare, for example, the more modern historically accurate biographies of St. Aloysius Gonzaga with the older ones. In particular, there seems to be danger in presenting people who have to pass their lives in secular pursuits, under active conditions, with the ideals of monastic existence.[84]

It is much better to choose ideal figures for some particular objective, like St. Aloysius for innocence of life, St. Mary Magdalen for penance, St. Ignatius for zeal, St. Therese for simplicity,[85] and so on. We repeat that there can be no duplication of personality and

---

[84] Rudolf Allers, M.D., *The Psychology of Character* (New York: Sheed & Ward, 1935), p. 198. Reprinted with permission of Sheed and Ward, Inc.

[85] "The little St. Therese of Lisieux, a saint of our own time, may be mentioned as an example of the second kind of aim—determination. She wanted above all else to be a child before God. Perhaps we could also say of the spirituality of her early life, which she herself has described for us, the religious ideal, which appealed to her, was that of a little daughter, who, enthusiastically adoring and loving her Father with boundless love, and absolutely inspired with confidence, allows herself to be guided entirely by Him and is on that account ready for any sacrifice which this guidance might demand. All this applied to her personal relationship with God. And she recognized that it was to be her life—task to exemplify in her own person this religious ideal, this 'Way of little souls' as she called it, for the edification of her fellowmen" (Johann Lindworsky, S.J., *The Psychology of Asceticism* [London: H. W. Edwards, 1936], p. 9).

the type or the manifestation of virtue in the concrete setting of an individual human being is necessarily modified by that setting, so that we have no longer the virtue itself, let us say of charity, but the virtue of charity as seen in someone, and that may or may not be attractive and imitable to a given individual at a given time.

The only universal ideal that is always useful and that is never faulty is that of our Lord. As the manifestation of God among men and consequently of infinite perfection, He is always attractive and always suitable as an ideal character for anyone. His virtues were without excesses and without defects, and the dominance of one virtue never caused the lessening of another.

There is a conclusion here for us. The person of Christ is the only sure concrete realization of an ideal. We can all afford to strive to be like Him because here there is no sacrifice of individuality. With this in mind He becomes an ideal for every state in life and for every situation. He should be presented not only in all the forms He took but in all those He might have taken and in all those He would take if He now walked our paths visible to outward eyes.

The Church, again, has sanctioned this idea by presenting Him as a child to children, as an adolescent to the young, as a man to the mature. In dealing with children we can show how He would have acted in their places. An excellent example of this pedagogical technique is in an illustrated serial that used to appear in a diocesan paper. In it the young Jesus was shown in typically modern garb and in typically modern life situations. Through this the young boy could actually visualize what his "ideal" would do on the baseball field, in camp, at school, at home, and so on. It reduced the thing from the abstract and the unreal to a tangible and attainable level and, paradoxically enough, that is the first requirement of every ideal.

What a far cry this is from the monstrous habit of distributing and honoring "holy pictures" that depict Jesus as an effeminate, emaciated weakling, very often with rouged lips and plucked eyebrows! Only the good will of those who use this strange means to encourage piety excuses the sacrilege. There seems to be an extraordinary idea abroad that *all* pictures of our Lord or our Lady are good pictures. As long as there is a halo on their heads!

Adults, for the most, suffer nothing worse than a development of bad taste from this traffic in the grotesque. But children! How can a boy form an attractive mental image of his Lord when the pictures of Him show a man he would be afraid to meet at night on a lonely road?

All the evidence of Scripture points to Jesus as a "he–man" — of powerful physique, of great strength, of commanding bearing. An emasculated approach to Christianity is giving Him to our children as a fop or an invalid. No wonder they are growing up thinking that He may be all right in His place, but they'd rather be like Mickey Mantle.

SECTION FOUR

FEAR

CHAPTER 12

FEAR AND ITS EXPLANATION

• • •

"A very successful engineer of forty–five years of age became a source of worry to his wife when he announced one evening 'I think they are going to get me.' Had his wife been trained in psychology she would have noticed that this statement did not really arise out of thin air, but that her husband's behavior had previously shown eccentricities in many respects. For instance, she might have noticed that he always looked up and down the street before leaving his office, that he had been pinching his left arm on awakening in the morning and before going to sleep, that the derogatory remarks that he had habitually made about certain business associates had increased in their frequency and in their virulence of late, that he had been sleeping poorly. After making the remark 'I think they are going to get me' the patient went into a panic of fear, broke down and cried, begged for his wife's protection, and lost all sensation in his left arm. It became quite obvious to the family doctor that the man had developed a mental illness, and he was sent to a hospital for psychiatric treatment.

Let us see what symptoms this man actually had. The outstanding symptom was the delusion of persecution. He had come to believe that his business rivals were plotting to ruin his business in two ways. In the first place they were going to spread malicious rumors about him, and in the second place, one of them had invented an electrical machine that by special waves would paralyze his left arm. With these delusions of persecution, however, were delusions of grandeur. As we have pointed out, the man was successful but probably not so successful as he desired to be. The rivals were persecuting him to prevent him from arriving at this great success. With the delusions there were disorders of perception. He knew they were persecuting him because voices told him so, i.e., he had hallucinations. There were disorders of sensation because he actually developed an anesthesia of the left arm, that he thought his rivals had brought about by an electrical machine. There were disorders of attention because he could not get these persecutory thoughts out of his mind and disorders of association because these fixed ideas caused him constant worry. Since he believed in both the delusions and the hallucinations he suffered paramnesic symptoms. He actually remembered the voices and he remembered noticing that Mr. Blank, his rival, whispered about him and gave him a mean look the last time they met."[86]

Treatises on psychology and psychiatry abound with cases similar to the one quoted above. We have chosen this one as an illustration of the far-reaching results of fear and anxiety in the human mind. In fact, experts tell us that fears, particularly hidden ones, are the greatest single source of neurotic behavior. Freud developed a great deal of his system around the idea of unfortunate events in childhood that are repressed because unpleasant, but that recur in disguised forms through the outgrowth of the anxiety they produce and that has never been lost.

[86] J. F. Brown, *The Psychodynamics of Abnormal Behavior* (New York: Mc-Graw-Hill, 1940), p. 108. Reprinted by permission of McGraw-Hill.

Although it is virtually impossible to separate the two in actual life situations, we cannot discuss in the same breath the fear that is best described as neurotic anxiety and fear on a conscious level. As we have already stated, separating this dual level of human motivation is one of the most real problems of the psychologist and philosopher of our day.

To avoid confusion as much as possible, we repeat our already adopted position—that we are speaking of fear (in this case) mostly on the conscious level. Examples like the foregoing one clearly indicate that neurotic anxiety goes much deeper—that it has its source and its breeding ground largely in the unconscious. But the necessarily limited role that we have taken upon ourselves does not include any attempt at the analysis of therapy at this level. This is a task for the professional depth psychologist.

At the same time we are convinced that an understanding—not so much of fear as of the antidote to fear—on the conscious level can also be of great help even where the fears go deep. We are all surrounded by anxieties and immersed in them, and a knowledge of certain guiding principles can help us all. Where they reach the point of neurosis, as above, then other and more direct therapy must be brought to bear.

Fear, worry, anxiety, call it what you will, on a conscious or semiconscious level needs no proof of existence. The famous psalm of the *Miserere* bemoans that "in sins did my mother conceive me."[87] The psychologist could paraphrase it to read "in fear and anxieties did my mother conceive me." It is one of the heaviest burdens of the human race. We worry about the past, we worry about the future. We worry if people don't like us and we worry if they do lest it is because we are not worth opposing. We worry about our

[87] Ps. 50:7.

health, our work, our finances, our children, and our friends. We even worry about worrying. And worry is just a concentration on one of our fears. So the existence of fear in our lives, in varying degrees, is established. Nor is there any doubt that fear or anxiety can contribute to psychological maladjustment. This may be the deep maladjustment that produces neurosis or psychosis or it may simply be an inability to face the total problems of life with sufficient assurance. Where neurosis begins is not, of course, a problem for us to discuss at this moment. But it is safe to say that a certain amount of neurotic anxiety is present in all our lives at different moments or in varying degrees. And this type of anxiety can prevent us from achieving our full possibilities.

The point in that we are interested here is what kind of therapeutic thinking can we present to eliminate or to reduce fear that is getting a little out of hand. Without any criticism of either the techniques or the good will of the psychologist we are convinced that a purely naturalistic approach to this problem is not sufficient. The science of psychology or psychiatry, as such, does not depend on theology or theological considerations. In this it holds common ground with all the other positive sciences. As a result, the delving into the unconscious, the rationalization of anxieties, their production at the level of consciousness in order that they may be faced and resolved, are all legitimate phases of psychotherapy. It is at the level of facing these anxieties or fears that we present some considerations.

And here of course we have a meeting place with those fears with which we are all too familiar: the fears in life that stalk abroad boldly, like how to meet the next payment on the house, how to face a serious operation, or even as simple a thing as a coming examination. The whole attitude toward life and death must for peace's sake have a permanent and a supernatural viewpoint. This cannot be produced by a purely naturalistic psychology. It is always intriguing to try to imagine the dialogue between a man condemned to face execution on the following morning and a psychologist or psychiatrist who has no belief in another world. How would the fears of the morrow be stayed in such a case? What comfort could be brought to this individual? Perhaps there are answers to this. They would be exceedingly interesting. For that matter, what arguments does the purely naturalistic psychologist use on himself when he catches himself worrying about death or what may be after death?

> To sleep, perchance to dream; aye there's the rub,
> For in that sleep of death what dreams may come
> When we have shuffled off this mortal coil
> Must give us pause.[88]

Finally there is that problem, that is more basically philosophical and theological than psychological, of the general origin of fear in man from the point of view of his race history; and in this connection even those who honestly reject the Christian explanation, that we are about to consider, admit that there is a hidden uneasiness, a wonder and a worry, a primordial feeling of guilt and anxiety that cannot be traced to the mere memories of childhood, but that reaches farther and deeper. A few put it down to race memory, a nebulous heredity, an ingenious but farfetched theory of the father–killing engraved on the consciousness of mankind. And they don't ever dream that perhaps they are closer to truth than they realize because they are touching with the tips of their fingers a truth or a series of truths that they pretend long since to have thrown overboard.

---

[88] William Shakespeare, *Hamlet, Prince of Denmark,* Act III, Scene I.

CHAPTER 13

CHRISTIAN ATTITUDE TOWARD FEAR

● ● ●

Theology is not concerned whether or not we are born with fears. But it does have an explanation of the basic insecurity that leaves the little one an open prey to these fears when they do come to him. Moreover, theologians and psychologists agree on the idea of "race memory," although the former give it another and different meaning. As Fr. Murphy writes:

> May it not be that, stored up in human nature and transmitted down through the ages is the effect of that primal offense that made man hide his face? Our First Parents heard the voice of the Lord God walking in paradise at the afternoon air; a voice that must have rolled like thunder over their guilty hearts and set every nerve aquiver in a manner which we, who bear the shame of their sinning, might well share. They hid themselves from the face of the Lord, amidst the trees of paradise. And the Lord God called Adam and said to him "Where art thou?" And he said: "I heard Thy voice in paradise and I was afraid."
>
> Here we see the original fear in humanity, aroused by the stentorian sound of the Almighty and risen from the realization of a fall from grace—a sense of guilt.

Psychologists are coming, more and more, to the finding of guilt of some kind or other as seminal to phobias; and the drama of that early garden of delights, so suddenly lost to man, bears them out. The guilty fear, Holy Scripture declares, when no man pursues; for when man has broken the law, there is always in his heart the sounding of conscience, which seems to be the echo of a godly voice, and also is there a feeling of insecurity, as if he had let go of a higher support and were miserably failing. The noises of breaking limbs, thunder and other sound–producing phenomena, which Watson mentions as causal of this major emotion in primitive men, were little in comparison with the warnings within himself. Before sin man feared nothing; after it, everything. The earth was cursed in his work, and everywhere he turned he met some reminder of the judgment he could not escape. Through him the race was conditioned in fear; and just as the babe trembles at external noises and the loss of support, so does the adult give way at the more significant bestirrings within him.[89]

Thus, Freud was closer to the truth than he knew. There was a killing of the father inasmuch as Original Sin was a blow leveled at the Father of all men and that had a certain objective infinity because it was an injury aimed at an infinite person, however little He could be reached by man's rebellion. And thus came with it, we maintain, the loss of original innocence. Since man no longer had the special protection of his Father and was in danger of sickness and death and was lost in ignorance, he began to fear. And in his heart of hearts was impressed a feeling of anxiety, an anxiety

[89] Edward F. Murphy, S.J., New *Psychology and Old Religion* (New York: Benziger Brothers, 1933), p. 113.

that weighed on the whole race.[90] This anxiety feeling must not be identified either with the unconscious guilt that can be recognized only indirectly in its effects, and that shows forth in patterns of self-punishment or with the guilt feelings that rise from the unconscious and that may be of neurotic origin. This latter type may be due to some hidden psychic imbalance or induced by a measurable factor such as the faulty attitude toward sex that some parents inflict on their children from an early age.

Nor is it precisely the sometimes entirely conscious and certainly salutary guilt that comes from a realization of wrong doing. It is the mysterious, universal uncomfortableness of the human race in which we all partake through human solidarity and that comes from the original dislocation of the universe in man's first and cataclysmic sin.

But whether it be this basic distress of the human race or the more palpable fears that are unavoidable in any life, we must seek the proper attitude toward fear.

It is already clear from the weaknesses inherent in the purely naturalistic psychological approach that a religious approach is necessary for the successful management of fear in one's life. It is to be noted that we say "management," not "suppression." We do so because the first contribution of the Christian attitude to fear is the clear-cut distinction between useful fear and harmful fear. The opposition between the two is evident even in a cursory reading of the New Testament. "Fear not, it is I," "Fear not, little flock," "True love casteth out fear," and many other similar texts indicate that there is a type of fear to be avoided. On the other hand we see that some fear is not only not harmful but necessary — "Fear him that can cast both body and soul into hell." "Fear is the beginning of wisdom."

---

[90] Donnelly's book, *The Bone and the Star,* already referred to, is a lengthy comparison between the two concepts of man's origin and psychological background: the naturalistic psychologist's and the Christian tradition.

In other words we are again on the same terrain as the psychologists who now admit the same distinction even though they often differ as to what things are fear worthy and what are not.

But the Christian distinction goes very deep. Let us consider what it is we should fear and how we should fear. Theologians distinguish three fears. The first is *slavishly servile* fear, and this is to be rejected because it is an insult to the love of God. The second is *servile* fear that is consonant with the beginning of love and through which God is feared because of His justice. This is acceptable because it is the lowest rung on the ladder of love, even though it is far from being a perfect state of mind. Finally there is *filial* fear that is compatible with the greatest love of God and the greatest peace of soul. Fr. Vann writes:

> But though this is far from the religion of servile fear, fear of another sort is still an essential element in it. It is fear which is the beginning of wisdom; without it we cannot be taught, we cannot grow; but it is not present only at the beginning. Beyond the completely servile fear of the slave there is the fear of the loving but as yet unreasoning child, and its fear is an element we cannot ignore or try to eliminate, though if we teach and train aright, it will pass as the child grows in grace and wisdom into the higher, freer, and reasoned obedience of the son, in which it becomes mainly or exclusively reverential. Beyond this again there is the fear, wholly identified now with loving awe, which is proper to the lover. The life of the spirit must follow these progressive steps from fear to fear. We shall never learn to love God aright unless we have learnt to sense His majesty, to know Him as terrible. But that same sense of awe is never left behind; it grows as wisdom grows. For it is simply the recognition of the abyss which lies between creature and

Creator; and it must grow in intensity as we come to realize more fully what infinity means. This fear, which is not only compatible with but an essential element in our divine sonship, is the condition of love as of wisdom; for it is what makes us teachable; and so we have to guard it and labour to deepen and intensify it, till it can become, in the end, a part of heaven's unending hymn of praise and glory.91

From our point of view such fear not only is compatible with a great peace of mind but actually constitutes its basis. Because we fear in this loving way we are teachable. Our mind is open to the movements of the Holy Spirit. Fear is one of the gifts of the Holy Spirit, and with it we are not in danger of losing the great gift of our union with God.

This last–mentioned idea is of the greatest importance to the psychology of the question. By fearing the proper object, God, in the proper way, we cleanse our souls of all other fears. We recognize the abyss between Him and us and our utter dependency on Him and our ability for evil. Our filial fear shows us that the only real loss would be that of God; consequently, *nothing else, however terrible, really matters*. We become free with the freedom of the children of God. No longer do we cling with feverish fingers and terrified hearts to the things of creation, even health or life itself. We are detached from all things; "God alone suffices."

So again we have driven home our point that only the saints are perfectly at peace psychologically. That is the spirit of mind that allowed St. Thomas to give his famous answer to the Figure on the cross who said to him: "Well hast thou written of Me, Thomas. What reward wilt thou have?" "Nothing save Thee, Lord." Here was

---

91 Rev. Gerald Vann, O.P., *The Divine Pity* (New York: Sheed & Ward, 1946), p. 35. Reprinted with permission of Sheed and Ward, Inc.

peace in poverty and possession: in poverty there could be no fear of loss, because Thomas possessed nothing of the world or cared not for what he possessed—or rather used; in possession, because he clung to the one thing that is everything.

By the same token the virtue of confidence is always the distinguishing mark of sanctity. We might say that confidence in God is the psychological fount of this gift of fear and its accompanying detachment. We cling to God, we love Him, and we know that He loves us. Consequently, we know that nothing can harm us, nothing is to be feared. We are at peace.

Witness that sense of sureness, of security, in the saints. It is the foolproof mark of sanctity. In the working of wonders it is really not so much the miracles themselves that should astound us as the matter–of–fact manner in which they are received by those who work them. Our Lord pointed that out when He said: "not stagger in his heart."[92] It is the key to moving the mountain.

To choose one illustration less known than most, we have the record of one who though uncanonized must still have been very close to God. It is Brother Joachim whose story is told by Fr. Raymond in *The Man Who Got Even With God.* His sister was on a visit to the monastery with a young son recently recovered from a serious pulmonary illness. A sudden downpour of rain threatened them while out walking. The holy monk took the child in his arms and sent his sister on ahead to the security of the monastery. Then he followed along at a more leisurely pace with the child, praying softly to God amid the thunder and the teeming rain. Arriving at the monastery door where the poor mother stood in an agony of fear and worry, the man of God handed her the child perfectly dry and smiling. And the point is that he met the bewildered amazement

<hr />

[92]   Mark 11:23.

CHRISTIAN ATTITUDE TOWARD FEAR

of his sister with the utmost calm, asking her why she was surprised that God should so take care of His little ones.

There is no greater or better cure for the worries that beset the heart and unsettle the mind than the virtue of confidence. It is the best possible approach to anxious minds to give them peace. And what is more, it can be taught as the purely logical outcome of the Christian belief. It is not a question of finding new doctrines or abstruse explanations. It is rather in taking our beliefs at their face value. Children are particularly adept at this, much more so than we adults.

The fact is that the virtue of confidence is based upon our belief in the omnipotence of God and God's love for us. We believe that God is all–powerful. We believe also that God loves us more than anyone else could. Now, when we really love a person there is nothing we would refuse if it would help him. Only *we* are limited in our power. God loves us; therefore, He wills to help us in everything. He is all–powerful; therefore, He is able to help us in everything. All we have to do is to put our hand in His hand and to go forth without fear. It is what Péguy calls "God's little hope."

> I said to the man at the gate of the year
> "Give me a light that I may tread safely into the unknown."
> And he replied
> "Go out into the Darkness
> And put your hand into the hand of God.
> That shall be to you better than light
> And safer than a known way." — Author unknown.

The Common Ground

Now we are in a position to be able to see how the Christian way is also a psychological way.

Let us consider first the fears of childhood origin, usually of the unconscious variety that return in disguised form. We have said that the psychotherapy involved in such cases is not within our competence. Yet there are certain pertinent factors with which we can deal. It is not possible to distinguish perfectly between cause and effect in these matters. In some cases fear is the result of some conduct factor in self or in others, but in many cases fear is the cause of the disturbance. Here is how Allers puts it:

> First of all it should be explained why we have given priority to a discussion of fear. There is no case of characterological anomaly either in children or in adults, no case of dissociation, as in neurosis, no case of difficult upbringing or of childish shortcomings, in which open or variously disguised fear does not lurk; it is a never–failing symptom of all faulty adaptation to the actual conditions of life. But only in part is fear a consequence of this lack of adaptation; it is to a far greater extent a cause of it. Here, again, we are faced with a vicious circle, whose nature we must grasp if a way out is to be found.
>
> It is not too much to maintain that in innumerable cases of difficult upbringing involving such features as stubbornness, excessive reserve, lying, rebellion against school, self–neglect and childish "criminality" — if this term is really applicable to the misdeeds of children — are at the bottom all founded on fear.[93]

In such a concatenation of causes we wish to achieve certain very limited objectives. First, we want to make readers unskilled in psychological thought aware that there may be deep psychological factors involved in mysterious or even incomprehensible conduct

[93] Rudolf Allers, M.D., *The Psychology of Character* (New York: Sheed and Ward, 1935), p. 156. Reprinted with permission of Sheed and Ward.

patterns. And these factors are very frequently at the unconscious level. Only the results show through. Second, we wish to establish that both in depth therapy and in the more simple aspects of helping in fears and anxieties of a more conscious origin, appeal must finally be made to a confidence and an assurance that is God-based.

The first objective may be brought closer by the examination of a typical case history.

> An attractive girl, age seventeen, came to the attention of a certain clinic as a voluntary case. For several years her parents had been concerned over the abnormal shyness which she exhibited in the presence of young men or boys. In the presence of members of the opposite sex, she would blush violently and lapse into a nervous silence after a few stammered remarks. Her behaviour was arrogant when she was with girls of her own age, and least confident in the presence of adult women. Since she was the daughter of a socially prominent family, the problem presented by this extreme shyness with boys became more and more serious as the year of her formal presentation to society approached. It was this consideration which finally led the parents to consult with the psychologist.
>
> The medical findings were negative. There was no organic disease apparent. In fact, the girl's physical health was decidedly above average. The social investigation revealed nothing in the home environment at the moment which would seem to be responsible for her mental condition. But social investigation did yield the significant fact that her shyness had developed quite suddenly three years before. The parents had no explanation to offer as to the possible cause of the condition.

> The psychologist talked with the girl in a friendly
> and informal manner. In the course of the conversa-
> tion it was observed that, while she discussed sports
> and school activities quite freely, she would invari-
> ably become emotional when the subject of boys was
> mentioned. After several talks the girl had become
> quite friendly with the woman psychologist and was
> by then looking upon her as a competent and sympa-
> thetic adviser. Little by little the following story came
> out. Three years before at a children's party the girl
> had been playing with some boys. In some manner
> she caught her fingers in a door when it was slammed
> shut. This caused the child such extreme pain that
> she became ill and vomited. The incident was quickly
> forgotten by everybody but the little girl herself, to
> whom it remained as a crushing misfortune. Although
> she tried not to think of it, the bitter memory was
> always there to be reinstated by the presence of boys.[94]

A case like this is the proper field of the psychologist. But a few
comments are in order for us here. The first lesson to learn is that
there was something very profound at the basis of the girl's fear. To
have bullied her or forced her might have been disastrous. We are
dealing here with the mystery of human personality and we must
enter it with respect. Man is complicated by his fears that are not
all of his doing. Even if they were, their adjustment requires tact
and patience and love. Abnormal fears of this kind should not be
met by scorn or reproach just because "we do not understand." As
a matter of fact that is to meet fear with fear.

Again we believe that when this anxiety has been diagnosed
and the full benefit of psychiatric or psychological treatment has

[94] Floyd L. Ruch, *Psychology and Life* (New York: Scott, Foresman, 1941),
pp. 144–145.

been brought to bear to make it conscious, an appeal to religious motivation can then prove of great help. Certainly, it is valuable to offer natural motivations, such as the need to put such a thing aside, the danger of future maladjustment and the spoiling of life, the realization that after all the incident was forgotten by everyone else and there was no longer any call for shame or embarrassment. But we have only to look into our own hearts to know that what we have said about a kind Providence and the acceptance of true religious values in life is really of far greater therapeutic value than any of these natural reasons. In particular, we insist that confidence in God aids us, children and adults alike, to ride over such crests of sorrow without being submerged by them.

And it is perhaps as good a moment as any to make mention of the psychological value of the Sacrament of Penance. So much has been said on this subject, and its relationship to psychotherapy is so obvious that we will not develop the theme. Here it is enough to point out that this is a God-given way to have every man face the innermost recesses of his conscience. If the sacrament is used right it is the source of great comfort. It will not prevent neurotic anxiety in some, nor will it prove a universal cure. Some have maintained that "the only psychiatric couch required is the confessional." This is an oversimplified view to which we have no temptation to subscribe. But for the adjustment of the ordinary man or woman it is psychologically invaluable. To keep in the forefront of our consciousness incidents we would rather forget until we have an assurance of pardon is a good prevention of future anxiety. Since many non-Christian psychologists have extolled the virtues and the benefit of confession from this point of view, we will say no more.

And what of the fears of an overtly conscious nature—or at least in which the stimulus is a clearly defined threat? These are the fears of our everyday life. Man is surrounded by the possibilities of disaster in the physical, the intellectual, and the moral spheres. In fact, security hangs by such a tiny thread that it is surprising that there is not even more fear than there is. Ignorance mercifully hides from us the volcanoes over which we sleep and the precipices on whose brink we wander. Unless such fears are abnormal, morbid, there is not much the purely naturalistic psychologist can say. If he says we are not going to be ill and suffer and lose our friends and die, then he lies. And as for the natural reasons for accepting such trials — there are not many. So we return to what we have said about "to care and not to care," to fear and not to fear. We fear the loss of God; we have certain natural emotional fears in the face of the lightning or the tornado or the surgeon's knife, but deep in our hearts there can be peace, "the peace of God, which surpasseth all understanding."[95] Fear is transformed. "Death is swallowed up in victory. Oh death, where is thy sting?"[96] Can natural psychology say that? Suffering and loss are the "momentary and light of our tribulation,"[97] because they are only temporary and we will recover all in God. "All that thy child's fancy pictures as lost, I have stored for thee at home. Rise, clasp My hand and come."[98] God loves us and watches over us. "Thou leadest, Oh Christ, all's well with the troopers that follow." And in proof of this, who are the serene and peaceful ones of this earth? Those who have left all things, who possess nothing and live in God. It is the only escape from fear. It is the great peace. *Pax magna!*

Free-Floating Fear and Scruples

There is a state of mind that is peculiarly difficult to define or to analyze because it touches on the area of neurotic anxiety and also

---

[95]   Phil. 4:7.
[96]   1 Cor. 15:54–55.
[97]   2 Cor. 4:17.
[98]   Francis Thompson, *The Hound of Heaven.*

on the area of religious motivation. Psychology describes a state of mind that is known as free–floating fear.

> In the phenomenon known as free–floating fear there is either no perceived stimulus for the anxiety (the individual is afraid but he does not know of what) or the stimulus changes rapidly. An individual may be afraid that his wife is going to die of cancer and upon being shown that this is unreasonable he will begin to worry about the stability of the bank in which he has an account, and when this is cleared up he becomes just as afraid that an automobile is going to run him down if he crosses Main Street.[99]

Anyone with experience in psychology or, for that matter, with any experience in dealing with the problems of other human beings, has encountered this type of anxiety. Very often it is a neurotic state or approaches one, and it requires the help of the professional psychologist. We are not trying to enter that domain as such, but we are interested in this state of free–floating fear where it touches upon religious living.

And this it does quite readily. Since this type of fear tends to settle upon the object that is most cherished or that is the area for the greatest concern, it is quite logical that in very religious people it should manifest itself in an exaggerated emotional worry about the things of religion. To a person with strong religious upbringing the concept of the loss of God for all eternity is the most appalling that can be mentioned. The commission of a grave sin is the subject of great concern and worry. Therefore, when, for one reason or another, such persons tend toward a state of morbid anxiety, they will tend likewise to make these subjects the aim of their particular fear.

---

[99] J. F. Brown, *Psychodynamics of Abnormal Behavior* (New York: McGraw–Hill, 1940), pp. 131–132.

In some cases, this is simply a form of neurotic anxiety and should be treated like any other neurotic anxiety. This is the work of a professional, as we have stated, and sometimes by resolving the difficulties, or even by some physical remedy, the person's condition is ameliorated and the "scruples" disappear. At the same time it would be far too sweeping to say that everyone suffering from scruples requires the aid of a psychiatrist, except in the general sense that we would all profit occasionally by the advice of these skilled professionals. There are states of scruples that arise from a real, though exaggerated, fear of the loss of God, or of spiritual damage, or that are caused at least in part by a temporary state of ill–health or worry, that will never come under psychiatric examination. The priest, the teacher, or simply the helpful adult, should have some concept of the spiritual therapy that can be brought to bear in these cases.

Setting aside the psychological causes of anxieties of this nature, let us examine the spiritual causes, because it is in this area that we would wish to apply an antidote. Scruples, speaking religiously, are partially caused or at least increased and complicated by a form of pride. This may be surprising to some because pride would seem to be the contrary. The scrupulous person is filled with self–accusation, seems to have no confidence in self, and in short considers himself in the words of Scripture "a worm and no man." But that is on the surface. Besides, it is bound up with the false concept of pride and humility that we have already mentioned. Pride is most adept at taking on the disguise of humility.

Scruples have their roots in pride because they consist precisely in not wishing to trust ourselves in the hands of God. We wish to have an absolute assurance of salvation where no such thing is possible. We wish to see ourselves in a state where grave sin cannot be committed and that is not part of God's plan for us in this world. And then, since we cannot achieve these things, we begin to worry.

In a way it is a form of the ancient Pelagian heresy that maintained that man could be saved by his own efforts. A scrupulous person is trying in a sense to save himself by his own efforts. He is trying to worry himself into Heaven. He is dissatisfied because his salvation is not in his own hands.

The treatment therefore must begin at this point. The scrupulous person must be led to understand that salvation is first of all from God although we must, of course, cooperate. But in his case the emphasis must be upon the contribution of God and therefore upon the goodness and the love of God for him. Very often at the basis of this type of fear lies a Jansenistic concept of God as the slave master who is trying to find us in sin in order that He can condemn us. When a person realizes that God "wishes that all men be saved" and that he is the object of God's individual love, then at least the door is open for relaxation and peace.

But this has to be translated into the practical field. And this is done under the aegis of religious obedience. In the treatment of scruples (on the level that we are now discussing) the only truly effective way is the acceptance of a personal spiritual director. In this there is a remarkable and interesting parallel with psychoanalytic treatment. At some stages of the treatment the patient is encouraged to transfer his dependence to his psychiatrist. In the religious treatment of scruples the same transfer must take part although in a different way. The *dirigé* must place himself entirely in the hands of a spiritual director and accept his decisions on all things pertaining to his religious life. Catholic theology justifies and approves such a transfer within limits. Thus the spiritual director can instruct the scrupulous person that he may, and indeed should, in all cases where an action is clearly not a sin, go forward without fear. There are many circumstances in which this assurance on the part of the director is necessary, because a scrupulous person may easily arrive at the point of confusion and of yielding to a form of temptation in which it is impossible for him even to receive Holy Communion. Thus, the spiritual director places him under strict obedience. This in itself is an antidote to pride. It is always difficult to yield the decisions of one's life to another. But in cases like these it is most essential and with it comes the blessing of God Himself who accepts this renunciation of one's own will and intervenes in the mind and the heart of the person so troubled.

And of course the great focus will be upon prayer. Prayer puts us in contact with God and makes us realize consciously how much we depend upon Him for every facet of our lives. In the scrupulous one this is a realization that is of the utmost necessity. By continuous prayer he takes the weight off his own shoulders and places that weight where it can be better borne, namely, on his Creator. Needless to say, since this is a trial and a suffering and a sickness like all others, God the All–Powerful can come to our assistance. Prayer, then, is the way to obtain surcease from these difficulties.

God expects us to take all the natural means at our disposal. We are in a sense a providence to ourselves and He will not help any except those who help themselves. But in the last analysis the mystery of the human soul is such that only God can treat it with a sure hand. Therefore what we have said of the treatment of scruples might well apply to the treatment of all mental illness. The person involved should, if possible, increase a thousandfold his prayer and his confidence in God. If he is unable to do so because of the state of his mind, then those about should substitute for him and that certainly includes his physician and his psychologist or psychiatrist. In medicine today the "team" idea is being extolled. What a pity that so often the team does not include the spiritual elements that would really make it a perfect unit. Where this can be achieved it should be an example for the whole world to observe.

Security

This brings us to what is perhaps the most popular concept in the world, the concept of security. Since the beginning of time man has sought for it. Adam sought for it in a false way. He wanted to become like God by his own strength. He wanted to take his security and place it in his own hands. He would not trust God.

Since Adam, the search has been even more frantic. Because of the fruit of Original Sin, the loss of God–clearly–known, man feels alone, isolated, and terrified. Therefore, his search for security has an element of frenzy and very often frustration. And as a result, it is presented to us in all the wrong places. A well–known bank recently advertised on a billboard: "There is no security in the world like a good bank balance." What must have been the thoughts of those refugees who came to America from the countries of Europe where they had had very good bank balances indeed. They must have thought bitterly of this type of security and how secure it is. Man has tried to place his security in every conceivable form of endeavor or achievement. The Tower of Babel is the supreme symbol of man's faulty attempt at security. And it all comes back to saying that there is no security outside God. Chesterton has said in the *Ballad of the White Horse* that a man only wins his wars when he has thrown his sword away. And so man only finds security when in a sense he throws away all human props. This does not involve imprudence but it does involve a great self–renunciation and a great understanding that only in God, as a final analysis, can we find a place upon which our feet can stand firmly. Even psychiatry, however legitimate and helpful, is a frail and uncertain reed.[100]

---

[100] Here is the way Ernest Haremann sums up the reliability of psycho–analysis: "All of this has led one prominent and conservative analyst to make this private evaluation: 'If what's troubling you isn't too serious and *if* you're lucky enough to go to one of the few analysts who seem to be good at what they're doing, and if you're a good patient and work hard, then maybe analysis can help you'" (*Life*, February 4, 1957, p. 77).

Hence, particularly in these matters in which we find ourselves assailed by fear, we must recognize that this is our common lot and that we must endure it, and the only surcease from our pain is in our trust in God. Even our Lord, sinless though He was, willed to feel fear in His soul. "Then he began to grow sorrowful and to be sad."[101] It is said that this so shocked the early Christians that they wanted to cut it from the first text of Scripture. But yet our Lord did feel fear in order that He might plumb human misery to the very depth. The same anguish caused Him to cry out, "My God, my God, why hast thou forsaken me?"[102]

Fear then is our common lot and the search for security our common condition. The problem is not to make the flight from fear an end in itself or to imagine that we can find security elsewhere but in those places where God has put it. The final answer can only be given by a total Christianity.

The sacraments, particularly Baptism, Penance, and Anointing of the Sick, are the balm that the Good Samaritan uses on the victim of the robberies of sin. The love of God, combined with contrition, or rather permeating contrition, raises the dead man, or cures the halt and the blind.

G. K. Chesterton has said that the principal reason among many reasons why he became a Catholic was that the Church was the only agency that openly claimed to forgive sins, and that could consequently take away the feeling of guilt that weighs us all down. Only here can we kneel at the feet of a qualified representative of Him whom we have offended and whose hand is heavy upon us, and hear from His lips, not a conjecture, not an exhortation, but the tranquil, majestic, and absolute assurance that our sins are forgiven us and our guilt taken away. Again, there is no other road to peace, security, and the only lasting freedom from fear given to man on the earth.

[101] Matt. 26:37.
[102] Matt. 27:46.

Conclusion

● ● ●

We do not pretend to have exhausted this subject. The field of psychology is as vast and as intricate as the nature of man himself and the field of theology and mysticism is as vast and as deep as the nature of God Himself. So the best we can hope to do is to touch with the tips of our fingers the truths that are hidden in the eternal mystery of the union between God and man.

Man is of the earth and has within him the terrible power of sin. There are possibilities so dark that we tremble at the very thought of them. The father of evil stands at our elbow to incite us to rebellion and to deeds of darkness. All of mankind is affected by the sin of Adam.

On the other hand, God created man out of love. "Good tends to communicate itself." God created man out of the goodness of His heart, the goodness that was so great it overflowed in the creative act. Not content with creating him in goodness, He has redeemed him in abundance. The redemption is an act of love far outreaching the comprehension of our minds; therefore, on the side of God is power that will not be denied, and that will not relinquish its loved ones until the last battle has been fought and the issue is decided for all eternity.

This has been an attempt to weld a few links between human knowledge in the psychological field and divine knowledge in the theological and mystical fields. We have tried to show that truth is one, that natural truth produced by the work of psychology is not at odds with the truth revealed by God and developed by His Church. On the contrary, we have tried to show that psychologists are arriving at many truths that we have known through God for many centuries, and at the same time we have tried to clarify our own knowledge of the Mystery of God within us by examining the undoubtedly valuable contributions of the psychologists to the field of human behavior. What stands out is this—true psychology without metaphysical bias or theological prejudice walks hand in hand with ascetical wisdom and the religious guidance of souls.

On the other hand, we must learn for once and for all that our revealed knowledge of the road to happiness is the safest and surest path. Happiness and adequate adjustment can come only in accordance with the principles set out by Christ for human behavior. Mental illness is not, in our view, incompatible with holiness. But holiness and *unnecessary* anxiety are strangers and it is often the latter that leads to maladjustment and neurosis.

"God shall wipe away all tears from their eyes: and death shall be no more, nor mourning, nor crying, nor sorrow"[103] is the promise of Heaven. Sanctity is an approach to Heaven, because it is an approach to God. Heaven is the possession of God through the Beatific Vision. Happiness on earth is the possession of God through faith. One is the beginning and the road to the other; consequently, only in faith and in love can we find the possession of truth and of good, that will satisfy us and give us the development of our faculties, the possibility of loving our fellow men, and freedom from unnecessary fear and anxiety.

The world is suffering indeed from a psychological malady; it is suffering from its separation from God, and there is only one therapy that can be universally prescribed and universally applied. That therapy is a humble yet glorious submission to the King of Peace enthroned in our hearts.

[103] Rev. 21:4.

About the Author

• • •

Father G. Emmett Carter (1912–2003) was cardinal archbishop of Toronto and an adviser to St. John Paul II. A participant in the Second Vatican Council, Fr. Carter worked to implement its decisions, especially in the areas of the Constitution on the Sacred Liturgy and the Constitution on Christian Education. A renowned author and Canadian educator, Fr. Carter helped reform the public education system for English-speaking Catholics in Québec.

Sophia Institute

Sophia Institute is a nonprofit institution that seeks to nurture the spiritual, moral, and cultural life of souls and to spread the gospel of Christ in conformity with the authentic teachings of the Roman Catholic Church.

Sophia Institute Press fulfills this mission by offering translations, reprints, and new publications that afford readers a rich source of the enduring wisdom of mankind.

Sophia Institute also operates the popular online resource CatholicExchange.com. *Catholic Exchange* provides world news from a Catholic perspective as well as daily devotionals and articles that will help readers to grow in holiness and live a life consistent with the teachings of the Church.

In 2013, Sophia Institute launched Sophia Institute for Teachers to renew and rebuild Catholic culture through service to Catholic education. With the goal of nurturing the spiritual, moral, and cultural life of souls, and an abiding respect for the role and work of teachers, we strive to provide materials and programs that are at once enlightening to the mind and ennobling to the heart; faithful and complete, as well as useful and practical.

Sophia Institute gratefully recognizes the Solidarity Association for preserving and encouraging the growth of our apostolate over the course of many years. Without their generous and timely support, this book would not be in your hands.

www.SophiaInstitute.com
www.CatholicExchange.com
www.SophiaInstituteforTeachers.org

Sophia Institute Press is a registered trademark of Sophia Institute.
Sophia Institute is a tax-exempt institution as defined by the
Internal Revenue Code, Section 501(c)(3). Tax ID 22-2548708.